A NO-NONSENSE STEP-BY STEP
GUIDE TO MASTERING EFFECTIVE
ESSAY WRITING

HOW TO
WRITE A
5-PARAGRAPH
ESSAY

- ✔ **Practical Study Skills**
- ✔ **Easy Exercises**
- ✔ **Simple Lessons**

for the Successful Student

SUCCESSFUL STUDENT PUBLICATIONS

ISBN: 979-8-9864302-0-1 (Paperback)

Table of Contents

Step 4: Polish and Shine

Step 5: Going Above and Beyond

Message for Teachers and Homeschooling Parents

Teachers

When you're standing in front of a class telling students they can have a blast while completing an assignment, you're often met with derision.

It can be exhausting trying to convince your students writing is fun. You could go on and on until you're blue in the face, and you still won't get your students to listen and engage with the material you are teaching.

It's no secret. Being a teacher is exhausting, especially when you spend endless weeknights and weekends lesson planning, prepping, and grading. There seems to be no end, and you must sacrifice your personal life and relationships to give your all to the role of being a teacher. The burnout is real, and that is OK.

Writing, especially coherent essay writing, is one of the most difficult concepts to teach. If you have pulled your hair out trying to create engaging lessons or have gone down the slippery slope of searching for "perfect" online, ready-made resources to no avail, then take a seat and relax. Let us do the heavy lifting, so you don't have to.

Use a fool-proof method on essay writing which *shows* your students the pleasure of the process. This book is here to make your life easier. It's a self-teaching guide, so give it to your students and let them take some control over their education. After all, when students have independence over their learning, you see the following:

- Increased motivation
- Higher academic performance
- More self-awareness of their academic strengths and weaknesses (Meyer et al., 2008)

Alternatively, you could use the content within this book to generate your lesson plan. You can even make photocopies of the exercises within this book and hand them out as worksheets! Any way you choose to use it, all the information your students need is right here!

Homeschooling Parents

Homeschooling is no walk in the park. Getting your child to sit down and do anything can be hard and convincing them to write an essay can be harder. It can sometimes cause anxiety and frustration for both of you.

It's challenging to maintain a structured teaching method and instill discipline when you're around each other 24/7. We hear you. You need resources that will engross and excite your child, particularly on topics they don't enjoy. Maybe then, some of the heat will be taken off of you!

You may be concerned your child struggles with essential writing techniques and they're falling behind some of their peers.

If your child lacks confidence, they may need some extra tools to give them a boost and remind them they *are* capable.

All of these are reasonable and normal frets. There are many hurdles young people must overcome in essay writing. This is what you need to focus on—supporting them to knock down these barriers.

P.S. We've provided an evaluation guide near the end of the book to help you gauge your student's or child's performance and apply a grade to their work.

Introduction

Get it down. Take chances. It may be bad, but it's the
only way you can do anything really good.
—William Faulkner, *A Faulkner Perspective*

Stresses for Students

Picture this. You're given the essay topic. Immediately, panic strikes—your breathing quickens, your heartbeat rises, and your palms get clammy. Next, the negative mindset kicks in. You tell yourself there's no way you can do it. You don't know enough. You think to yourself, *Why didn't I pay attention in class?*

By the time you actually write the thing, you're so stressed you can't think straight. Does this sound about right?

Maybe that's not it. Perhaps you hate essay writing because you just think it's plain dull. Whether you get anxious or bored, you're not alone. Most people dread essay writing for one reason or another.

But it doesn't have to be this way. Stress and sleepy eyes aren't what we want here. What you need: simple steps and deep breaths.

Non-Native English Speakers

What if English isn't your first language? Essay writing is hard enough for native speakers, let alone when you're tackling a language barrier, too.

What are the main problems?

1. English isn't written in the same way it's spoken. This causes all sorts of confusion when you're asked to write an essay.
2. Essay writing isn't like sending a text or writing a letter; it has different rules that can be difficult to understand.

3. It's quite a long process, and it can be exhausting if you're attempting to understand the language while also trying to write a perfect essay (North Carolina State University, 2021).

But don't worry! This guide is jam-packed with lessons everyone can understand.

We've given you easy-to-follow, step-by-step instructions that will support you through every part of essay writing. We leave nothing out! By the end of it, you'll be able to write a flawless English essay as if you've been doing it your whole life.

Returning Students

Have you been out of the game for a while? Feeling rusty? Well, shake off those cobwebs and get writing! Not writing for a time doesn't mean everything you've learned is lost or that you're incapable.

However, it's normal to have concerns. Maybe you're worried that all the rules have changed since you left school. You might be stressing out because you don't think you can get back into the swing of things.

Are you worried that since now you have a lot more going on, and you won't be able to fit in essay writing?

That's where we come in. This guide is filled to the brim with helpful tips and tricks to get you back into the rhythm of essay writing. What's more? We teach you essay writing doesn't have to be a long, arduous task, and we give you techniques to speed up the process.

This guide will hopefully spark some pre-existing knowledge. If not, you'll learn something new! Win, win.

What Makes Writing Essays Tricky?

For one, they can be tedious. They often take a lot of time, and they take effort. If you're an expert at putting off work, you may struggle even to sit down and get started.

Chances are, you're focusing on the wrong things. It's all too easy to set your heart on earning an excellent grade or making others proud. These rewards are *extrinsic*. They won't motivate you to pick up that pen or open that laptop.

Instead, try focusing on the enjoyment of writing itself (*intrinsic* rewards). In other words, stay thinking about the current moment, not the future prize. Once you start this, all those other rewards are likely to follow.

Another common hiccup is telling yourself you can't do it. Thinking in this way assumes your talents are set. This is called a *fixed mindset*. It's the belief you're either naturally good at something or not, and this can't change (Dweck, 2017). This simply isn't true!

Thinking in this way could be what's holding you back. It may cause you to

- avoid challenges because you worry you'll fail,
- believe practicing and putting in the effort is pointless,
- give up easily,
- be jealous of other people's success, and
- feel hurt when you receive feedback (Ackerman, 2021).

It's better for your writing (and your sanity!) if you have a *growth mindset*. This is all about remembering that your intelligence and talents can grow (Dweck, 2016). Like they say, practice makes perfect!

So, how can a growth mindset help you? Well, students who think in this way typically do the following:

- Get better grades
- Show more confidence (Curtis, 2019; Dweck, 2016)
- Have more motivation
- Learn better
- See challenges as a way to improve, not as a risk of failure (MacArthur & Moxley, 2020)

It's all about saying, "I can do this," rather than immediately believing you can't. This isn't easy, especially if you're used to having a fixed mindset. It's common to struggle with confidence when you're learning. After all, writing *is* hard, and there's a bunch to remember.

By following this guide and using the helpful step-by-step instructions, you will gain the confidence you need to think more positively about essay writing!

Just remind yourself to focus on enjoying the process and to keep practicing.

What's This Book About?

This book breaks down all the difficult parts of essay writing into simple, straightforward steps. You'll learn about writing challenges, such as creating an exciting introduction and a thoughtful thesis statement. We'll also venture into the different types of essays, so you can perfect each one.

You'll uncover ways to keep yourself chill while writing stellar essays. You'll even learn to enjoy the process! We provide exercises with answers to get you involved and allow you to check your hard work along the way.

We will also introduce you to outlining techniques and graphic organizers to make writing an ace essay easy.

The Steps

When a song comes on, and everyone knows the moves but you, terror creeps in. Don't let that be you in essay writing. Just like dance moves, you can break essay writing down into steps. We've done this for you!

There are five main steps, which the chapters of this guide follow:

1. Building a Foundation
2. Prewriting
3. Drafting
4. Polish and Shine
5. Going Above and Beyond

Chapter 1 ("Laying Out the Foundation") focuses on the first step. Here, we run through what a five-paragraph essay is and its importance. We talk about basic essay structure.

The second step, *Prewriting*, is covered in Chapters 2 and 3. Chapter 2 looks at planning. Here, you'll pick a topic, make sure you understand it, and identify your target audience. You'll learn how to brainstorm and research your topic, how to state your points confidently, and how to write effective thesis statements.

Chapter 3 is all about organization. Here, we look at outlines and graphic organizers to speed up the writing process, so you're not stuck writing this essay forever!

Next, in Chapter 4 we discuss the third step, *Drafting*. This section goes over every part of the essay. We talk about grabbing the reader's attention, getting your points across clearly, and backing your claim up with trustworthy research. You'll also learn how to wrap this all up in a compelling conclusion.

In Chapter 5, we talk about how to *Polish and Shine* your essay, the fourth step. It has three sections:

1. Revise
2. Edit
3. Proofread

This is the chapter that will make the difference between a good essay and a great one. It has all the information you need to make your essay really shine!

The fifth and final step, *Going Above and Beyond*, is a bonus. We cover this in Chapters 6 and 7. Chapter 6 goes over the different types of essays you're sure to come across and gives you a detailed explanation on how to tackle each one. You will use the basic structure and process of writing a five-paragraph essay learned in Chapters 2-5 and apply it to the different essay types we go over in Chapter 6.

In Chapter 7, we look at boosting your creativity, finding your voice, and reflecting on all that you have achieved.

It's All About the Layers

Looking at the chapters closely, you'll see plenty of smaller, bite-sized steps (called *lessons*) within each bigger goal. We've designed it this way, so you can keep having little wins throughout the book.

It may be tempting to skip past one section if you're only particularly worried about one area. Don't do it! Every step builds on the one before, and the only way to achieve a fantastic essay is to follow them one after the other.

Why This Guide?

If you're like most, you've tried many resources with no success. This guide provides something slightly different. It takes the drab and the dreary and makes it exciting and inviting.

To learn an "uninteresting" topic, you need simple language, easy steps, and someone who knows what they're talking about!

We are Successful Student Publications, a team of ambitious collaborators pioneering the world of writing by offering easy-to-use and accessible information for students and individuals of all proficiency levels to improve their writing skills. We provide books to guide students (like you!) through topics many people find tricky.

We've pinpointed what's needed to triumph in essay writing through extensive research, working with both students and teachers.

So, we've created a guide to help everyone achieve their best, whatever their age or grade. We're not called Successful Student Publications for nothing! We want all students to succeed.

Our easy-to-follow, step-by-step instructions and comprehensive resources will help you feel more confident about essay writing, and you might even discover you enjoy it! Everything you need is in one place—within these pages.

STEP 1

Building a Foundation

STEP 1

CHAPTER 1

Laying Out the Foundation

Have you ever tried to build a tower out of paper? Whether you have or have not, you are probably curious about why we are mentioning this random activity in a book about essays. The challenge requires you to construct a tower, as high as you can, with only paper. That is essentially the only rule. When students participate in this challenge, their towers often look very different from each other. Even though they are all given the same materials—several sheets of paper—their end products are not the same. Some students fold the paper, some students roll it up, and some tear it into pieces, all trying to complete the challenge with a slightly different approach.

There is one thing all the towers have in common:

A foundation.

No matter how tall or wide the towers are, they all have a solid foundation at the bottom that holds them in place. Without this foundation, the towers are doomed to fall from the start. Imagine trying to build one of these towers in midair. Unless it defies the laws of gravity, it would collapse to the ground as soon as you let go.

Now, imagine trying to write a five-paragraph essay without a solid foundation. You may create something that looks good, but take a step back. Your essay will look very different. Without a foundation, you wouldn't even know where to begin. Before tackling the essay, you need some knowledge on what a five-paragraph essay actually is. You also need to know its components!

Rather than throwing you into the deep end, this chapter is here to help you dip your toes in the water. We'll just touch on things here. The later chapters will explore everything in much, much more detail! Let's begin with *why* learning to write a five-paragraph essay is important.

Why Should You Learn How to Write a 5-Paragraph Essay?

You might be thinking, *Why do I have to learn how to write a five-paragraph essay? I'm never going to write one outside of school anyway.*

We hear you. But frankly, this is an outdated way of thinking. The five-paragraph essay is absolutely applicable to different areas of your life, and you need to understand why.

Writing any essay strengthens your research and critical thinking skills. These are two skills you will need no matter where you go in life. You will need to discover and be open to learning new information, process and understand information, and make informed decisions based on what you have learned.

In today's day and age, with a vast array of information at your fingertips, it is also important to know how to research and *filter* information. You need to determine what information is reliable, and knowing how to write a five-paragraph essay helps you sharpen this skill by putting it into practice.

Essay writing also gives you a way to communicate with an audience by providing a platform to express your thoughts, beliefs, and opinions. To communicate with an audience effectively, you must learn how to use words effectively and relate to your audience.

You'll come to realize it is not possible to communicate with everyone in the same manner and tone. You need to communicate with people in a way which makes sense to them or else you may not get the response you want.

Now, it is unlikely you will write your parents a five-paragraph essay to convince them to buy a dog or send your boss a five-paragraph essay explaining why you should get paid more. And even if you decide to write an essay, it may not end up being exactly five paragraphs. However, learning how to write a five-paragraph essay *now* helps prepare you for those situations. You may find yourself asking, "How will I convince my parents to buy a dog if I don't know where to get one?" or "How will I ever get paid more if I don't know how to show my worth?" These types of questions, believe it or not, will become much easier to answer as you develop your research and communication skills through ample practice with five-paragraph essays.

As you can see, there are endless ways learning how to write a five-paragraph essay may be beneficial to you and may be applicable for years to come. Keep this in mind, and it will keep you motivated for the rest of the book!

What Exactly is a 5-Paragraph Essay?

A five-paragraph essay is a form of prose writing that follows an organized structure composed of five distinct paragraphs: an introduction, three body paragraphs, and a conclusion (Fleming, 2019a). Let's look at the table for an overview.

What is it called?	What is it?	Why is it important to me?
Introduction	The first paragraph of your essay	You need to grab the reader's attention and introduce your main ideas. You will also present your thesis statement with three distinct points.
Body paragraphs	The three middle paragraphs of your essay	You need to present your ideas and expand on them with evidence and analysis.
Conclusion	The final paragraph of your essay	You need to remind the reader of your main ideas and provide a summary of what you've discussed in the rest of your essay. It should connect back to your introduction.

As the table mentions, the introduction is the first paragraph of your essay. It sets the stage for the rest of your essay by grabbing the reader's attention with a captivating hook, introducing your main ideas with well-developed background information, and stating a three-point thesis statement which outlines the points you will talk about in the subsequent three body paragraphs.

Each body paragraph will cover one of the three points from your thesis statement. You will start with a topic sentence that tells the reader what the main idea of the paragraph is. Then, you will follow up the topic sentence with supporting sentences, evidence, and analysis.

Lastly, you have the conclusion. The conclusion is usually a short paragraph that rephrases the thesis statement and summarizes the main ideas from each body paragraph. Its purpose is to close off the essay with key takeaways and a final message for the reader. You should not introduce new ideas in this paragraph (The Writing Center, 2009).

Don't worry if this seems overwhelming right now. We are just briefly going over the main components of a five-paragraph essay to give you a sturdy foundation to work from. If you are not familiar with some of the terms mentioned, don't fret! You'll become familiar with these terms as we move along in the book.

In the coming chapters, everything will be broken down step by step into manageable pieces that are easy to understand. Next, let's go over how this book is organized, so you can get the most out of it.

The Basic 5-Paragraph Essay Blueprint

Now you should have a preliminary understanding of the different components of a five-paragraph essay. This will make the coming chapters a bit easier to understand and absorb.

Chapters 2-5 are dedicated to providing you with an organizational *blueprint* of the basic five-paragraph essay. What this means is you will learn how to properly plan for and write a five-paragraph essay through a step-by-step process. You will also learn how to edit, revise, and proofread your essay to perfection. These are the most rudimentary steps you need to master before moving onto more complex pieces of essay writing as you advance in your career as a student.

Once you have finished going through Chapters 2-5 and have a grasp of the concepts, you will soon come to realize this preparatory blueprint carefully lays out a solid structure and framework that can serve as the *basis* for many, specific types of essays and literary works (Zile, 2006, pp. 4–5).

That is when Chapter 6 comes into play, and things get a little spicy! You will use the basic five-paragraph essay blueprint and apply it to the different essay types we go over in Chapter 6.

There are many kinds of essays which are more focused, elaborate, and layered than the basic five-paragraph essay, and you will likely get more exposure to these different types of essays and literary works as you mature as a student and take on more complex writing assignments. For the purposes of this book, we will only touch on a few different types of essays in Chapter 6.

To make sure it is not too much of a shock later on, let us briefly go over the four different kinds of essays we explore in Chapter 6:

Type of Essay	Description
Expository	Serves to explain and elaborate on a topic using factual information
Narrative	Serves to tell a story with a moral, usually pulling from life events
Descriptive	Serves to provide a detailed description about a place, object, situation, person, character, or event. Uses descriptive words to paint a picture in the reader's mind.
Persuasive	Serves to persuade or convince the reader of the author's viewpoint.

 Study Skill: Do not skip ahead in this book. Every lesson builds on the one before. Follow through on each step to ensure a full understanding of all concepts.

We're not going to provide any more information than that right now. Why? Getting started can be overwhelming, and we want to make it as simple as possible. It's easy to get lost in the weeds of every single detail. Taking a step back and looking at the bigger picture is sometimes the best thing you can do.

As you head into the rest of this book and start writing your five-paragraph essay, we hope the process will be a little easier than trying to build that high tower. We've given you a head start by giving you a foundation of knowledge about five-paragraph essays. Throughout the following chapters, we will incrementally provide you with the content and materials you need to write an essay. Just as each one of those paper towers is one-of-a-kind, your essay will also be unique. We want you to take what you learn in this book and apply it in your own creative way. There's only so far rules and guidelines can take you. Throughout the entire writing process, think about yourself and take ownership of everything you do. This is your essay, and you will make it amazing.

Chapter 1 Comprehension Quiz

Instructions: Circle the best answer.

1. **Why should you learn how to write a five-paragraph essay?**
    a. It strengthens your critical thinking skills.
    b. It helps you practice communicating with an audience through writing.
    c. It strengthens your research skills.
    d. All of the above

2. **What is the purpose of the introduction?**
    a. To grab the reader's attention and introduce your main ideas
    b. To present your thesis statement
    c. To conclude your essay
    d. Both A and B

3. **What are body paragraphs?**
    a. The three middle paragraphs of your essay, where you present your ideas
    b. The first and last paragraphs of your essay
    c. There is no correct answer.
    d. Body paragraphs are another name for conclusion paragraphs.

4. **What is the purpose of the conclusion?**
    a. To introduce your thesis statement
    b. To remind the reader of your main ideas and provide a summary
    c. To provide evidence and analysis
    d. To provide background information

5. **What is the basic five-paragraph essay blueprint?**
    a. A blueprint that lays out a floor plan for the construction of a house
    b. None of the answers are correct.
    c. A map with drawings that tells you how to structure a five-paragraph essay
    d. A solid structure and framework that can serve as the basis for many, specific types of essays and literary works

Chapter 1 Comprehension Quiz

Instructions: Circle the best answer.

6. Can the basic five-paragraph essay blueprint be applied to other types of essays?
      a. No
      b. Maybe
      c. Yes
      d. None of the above

7. What is the purpose of an expository essay?
      a. To convince the reader and sway them to agree with your viewpoint
      b. To paint a picture with vivid words and rich description
      c. To tell a story from relevant life experience
      d. To explain a topic using factual information

8. What is the purpose of a narrative essay?
      a. To convince the reader and sway them to agree with your viewpoint
      b. To paint a picture with vivid words and rich description
      c. To tell a story from relevant life experience
      d. To explain a topic using factual information

9. What is the purpose of a descriptive essay?
      a. To convince the reader and sway them to agree with your viewpoint
      b. To paint a picture with vivid words and rich description
      c. To tell a story from relevant life experience
      d. To explain a topic using factual information

10. What is the purpose of a persuasive essay?
      a. To convince the reader and sway them to agree with your viewpoint
      b. To paint a picture with vivid words and rich description
      c. To tell a story from relevant life experience
      d. To explain a topic using factual information

STEP 2

Prewriting

STEP 2

CHAPTER 2

Planning the Perfect Essay

This chapter is part of Step 2: Prewriting. Follow these eight lessons, and you'll be off to a great start planning your essay:

If you've already been given your essay topic, you should still read through this lesson.

Lesson 2.1: Choosing Your Essay Topic

We've reached the first step in this chapter: choosing the topic of your essay.

Everything starts with an idea! Think about your phone (if you have one). It didn't magically come about; someone came up with an idea of how it would look and what it would do. If we didn't have people cooking up new ideas, phones might still look like this!

Writing an essay is no different. It needs to start as an idea. You then turn this big idea into a topic by making it more specific. Don't worry; we'll coach you through this!

It's OK if you find this task overwhelming. Most people do. In fact, there are two common problems people have when picking a topic:

1. The topic isn't interesting.
2. The topic is too big.

We'll go through each of these dilemmas and show you how to avoid them!

Interesting = Easier!

When it comes to deciding on your topic, it's good to choose something that excites you and you want to learn more about.

You'll be a lot more motivated to write your essay (and do it well!) if you actually enjoy the topic you're writing about (Lo & Hyland, 2007).

Being interested in what you're learning has many benefits:

- Better focus
- More energy when learning
- Improvements in academic performance
- Increased motivation to dig deeper and learn more (Harackiewicz et al., 2018)

So, pick a topic that excites you and witness these positives for yourself!

Too Much Information!

It's important to remember you're only writing five paragraphs. You can only cover a small topic (Arquilevich, 1999, pp. 8–9).

Say you want to write about America. That's one big topic to cover, so you may be flooded with information when you go to research it. How about the United States? You would find it hard to write about all 50 states in just five paragraphs. Choosing one state, like Massachusetts, might be easier to write about, but it's still not specific enough. We can dig into the history of Massachusetts and write about a specific event. How about the Boston Tea Party? Now that's a topic!

In the diagram, we show the stages of turning your big idea into a specific topic. Imagine you're up at the top of the vines, wanting to get down. The thing is, there are so many vines where you are, you can barely see the ground!

To get to the ground, you need to travel down the vines, which get smaller and smaller as you go.

Just like the vines, when deciding your topic, you start with a big subject where there's an enormous amount of information. You need to make this subject smaller and smaller to get to your essay topic.

If you need inspiration, check out our "universe" example.

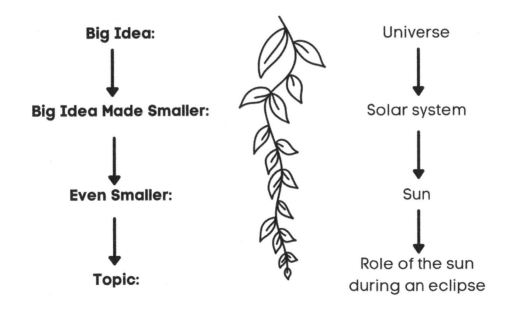

Big Idea:
↓
Big Idea Made Smaller:
↓
Even Smaller:
↓
Topic:

Universe
↓
Solar system
↓
Sun
↓
Role of the sun during an eclipse

Study Skill: A small topic is what we want, but not too small! Choose a topic you can still write five paragraphs about. Check this by searching your topic on the internet. If very little information comes up, pick something else!

From Topic to Prompt

Once you've narrowed your big idea down into a topic, there's one more step to take. For your topic to be essay ready, you need to transform it into a prompt. A prompt is a question or statement your essay answers. Questions are what most people use and what we recommend, but if a great statement pops into your head, brilliant! Use it.

If you pick a statement, make sure it includes words like "explain," "compare," or "contrast." These are called command words, and they will make your life easier when it comes to writing your essay. We will go over command words in the next lesson.

Going back to our example about the United States, a good prompt in the form of a question could be: What are the favorite foods of people living in Massachusetts? A good prompt in the form of a statement could be: Describe the favorite foods of people living in Massachusetts.

Let's use the topic from the earlier example to show you how to go from topic to prompt:

Topic: Role of the sun during an eclipse

Prompt: Explain the role of the sun during an eclipse.

There is more than one way to write a prompt. Here are a few more options to show you what they could look like:

Option 2: What is the role of the sun during an eclipse?

Option 3: Describe the role of the sun during an eclipse.

Option 4: What is the role of the sun during an eclipse? Explain your reasoning.

Lesson 2.1 Exercise: Big Idea to Prompt

Instructions: Work down each column in the tables below, filling in the blank boxes from big idea to prompt. Use the "music" example as a guide. In the last table, write some of your own big ideas.

①

Big Idea	Music	Food	Sports
Big Idea Made Smaller	Music genres	Fruit	
Even Smaller!	Pop music		
Topic	The best current pop artist		The most popular non-contact sport in the United States
Transform Your Topic into a Prompt	Question: Who is the best current pop artist? Statement: Explain who the best current pop artist is.	Question: What are the benefits of eating berries? Statement: Describe the benefits of eating berries.	

②

Big Idea	Hobbies	Technology	Education
Big Idea Made Smaller			
Even Smaller!			
Topic			
Transform Your Topic into a Prompt			

17

Lesson 2.1 Exercise: Big Idea to Prompt

Instructions: Work down each column in the tables below, filling in the blank boxes from big idea to prompt. Use the "music" example as a guide. In the last table, write some of your own big ideas.

③

Big Idea	Countries	Movies	Science
Big Idea Made Smaller			
Even Smaller!			
Topic			
Transform Your Topic into a Prompt			

④

Big Idea			
Big Idea Made Smaller			
Even Smaller!			
Topic			
Transform Your Topic into a Prompt			

Lesson 2.2: Getting a Grip on Your Prompt

Have you ever tried playing a new sport without knowing the rules? Well, essay writing is like that if you don't understand your prompt.

If you haven't come up with the prompt yourself, pay extra attention here. You may find it harder to understand if you haven't chosen it.

Prompt: the question or statement you need to answer in your essay

Take a look at the definition of a prompt shown above. When trying to understand your prompt, you need to ask yourself the following:

1. What is the topic of the essay?
2. What am I being asked to do?

Luckily, every prompt has keywords you can pick out to help you understand what it's asking for. There are two types of keywords:

- Subject words
- Command words

Subject words tell you what you need to write about (the subject). Command words tell you what you need to do. Look out for words like "describe," "compare," and "analyze."

Study Skill: Try highlighting the subject and command words in your prompt using two different colors. This will remind you what you need to do when writing your essay.

Command words, in particular, can be tricky to understand. Take a look at the table. It shows you the type of command words you might come across and what they're asking you to do (Matthews, 2020, pp. 10–11).

Compare	Show how two or more things are similar.
Contrast	Show how two or more things are different.
Explain	Write in detail about the topic. Imagine the reader knows nothing about it. What are the most important things to tell them?
Describe	Give a detailed description of the topic.
Analyze	Break your topic down into smaller parts and look at these in detail. Ask "why" and "how."
Discuss	Write your point of view and give evidence for this.

Here's an example of a very simple essay prompt with the subject and command words picked out for you.

Essay Prompt: Discuss basketball.

Subject Word: basketball

Command Word: discuss

It's important to remember subject words can also be phrases, not just one or two words. Here's an example:

Analyze the effects of climate change.

For this prompt, the subject words would be "the effects of climate change." This means you're looking at the impact of climate change rather than just looking at climate change in general. The command word here is "analyze."

Here's another example:

Essay Prompt: Describe the water cycle and why it is essential to life on Earth.

Subject Words: the water cycle and why it's essential to life on Earth

Command Words: describe

Study Skill: If your prompt doesn't have any command words, don't panic! Essay prompts can be sneaky like that sometimes. In these cases, assume the prompt is asking you to explain your thoughts (Matthews, 2020, p. 10).

Example:

Essay Prompt: How does eating fruit help your skin?

Subject Words: how eating fruit helps your skin

Command Words: No command word. Explain your thoughts on how eating fruit helps your skin.

Clashing Phrases

Sometimes, your prompt will contain a phrase with two words that oppose or *clash* with one another by asking you for **different** things. We call these *clashing phrases*. It's important that you are easily able to identify these phrases so you fully understand your prompt.

Here are some examples of possible clashing phrases within your prompt:

- Advantages **and** disadvantages
- Positives **and** negatives
- Pros **and** cons
- Compare **and** contrast
- Benefits **and** drawbacks
- For **and** against
- Similarities **and** differences

*This is not an exhaustive list of all existing clashing phrases.

As you can see, clashing phrases ask you for two sides of an argument. For example, if you see "advantages **and** disadvantages" in your prompt, you know you are being asked to consider the upside *and* downside of something. That's what makes these phrases special when analyzing your prompt.

Pay close attention to the word "and" in these phrases. If you see the word "or" instead of "and," this is no longer a clashing phrase because you are not being asked to consider two sides of an argument. The word "or" implies that you consider *one* side while the word "and" implies that you consider *two* sides.

You may have noticed that "compare and contrast" is on this list of *clashing phrases*. Let's not forget, however, that "compare" and "contrast" (as individual words) are also command words, which we discussed earlier in this lesson. In every other case, a clashing phrase is part of the subject words in a prompt (Matthews, 2020, p. 15).

Let's look at an example:

Essay Prompt: Describe the benefits **and** drawbacks of brushing your teeth.

Subject Words: the <u>benefits and drawbacks</u> of brushing your teeth

Command Word: describe

In this example, "benefits and drawbacks" is a *clashing phrase*, so we have underlined it. The phrase "benefits and drawbacks" is also part of the subject words.

In this next example, you'll observe that "compare and contrast" can be both a *clashing phrase* and the command words of the prompt.

Essay Prompt: Compare **and** contrast the seasons of the year.

Subject Words: the seasons of the year

Command Words: <u>compare and contrast</u>

*The phrase "compare and contrast" is underlined because it is also a clashing phrase in this prompt.

Lesson 2.2 Exercise: Picking Out Subject Words and Command Words

Instructions: Pick out the subject and command words for each essay prompt, then write down what each command word is asking you to do. If there are no command words, write "no command word." Underline any clashing phrases you find.

1

Essay Prompt
Explain the <u>similarities and differences</u> between American and English culture.

Subject words
the similarities and differences between American and English culture

Command word(s)
explain

What is the command word asking you to do?
to write in detail about the topic

2

Essay Prompt
Describe the life cycle of a frog.

Subject words

Command word(s)

What is the command word asking you to do?

3

Essay Prompt
Which historical events triggered the American Revolution?

Subject words

Command word(s)

What is the command word asking you to do?

23

Lesson 2.2 Exercise: Picking Out Subject Words and Command Words

Instructions: Pick out the subject and command words for each essay prompt, then write down what each command word is asking you to do. If there are no command words, write "no command word." Underline any clashing phrases you find.

---

(4)

Essay Prompt
Compare and contrast the effects of eating healthy food versus junk food.

Subject words

Command word(s)

What is the command word asking you to do?

---

(5)

Essay Prompt
Describe the effects of smoking on physical health.

Subject words

Command word(s)

What is the command word asking you to do?

---

(6)

Your Essay Prompt

Subject words

Command word(s)

What is the command word asking you to do?

Lesson 2.3: Identifying Your Audience

What Audience?

You now know what your prompt is asking you to do. The next step is thinking about whom you're writing the essay for. Who is your target audience?

Audience: the people (or person) your essay is directed toward

When writing an essay, it's easy to forget you're writing *to* someone. This is an important thing to remember if you want to write a great essay. But why?

Identifying your audience will help you do the following:

→ Decide what vocabulary to use in your essay

If you're writing to your friends, the words you use may be casual (aka informal). You may even use some slang words. If you're writing to your teacher, you will need to use more serious words (aka formal).

→ Choose the tone of your essay

Tone is the writer's attitude toward the reader. For example, if you were trying to persuade the reader, you may use a lot of command words that tell them what to do.

Who Is Your Audience?

If your teacher has given you the prompt, they're likely your audience. However, this might not always be the case. It would help if you thought about who your prompt *relates* to.

Say you're writing a persuasive essay, trying to encourage your classmates to raise money for charity. Here, your audience is your classmates, and you need to use solid and convincing words because you're trying to get them to follow your instructions.

If you're writing your essay for a competition or a blog, you'll have a bigger audience (Arquilevich, 1999, p. 21). In this case, you may want to consider the following specific information about your audience:

- Age
- Gender
- Background
- Interests
- Beliefs
- Education level

Thinking about these factors helps you adjust your writing style so your essay entices the reader.

Lesson 2.3 Exercise: Writing for Different Audiences

Instructions: Match up the writing samples with their audiences using the list of audiences provided.

Writing Samples

1. Can we please buy a bigger house so my sister and I can have separate bedrooms? I don't want to share anymore. I'm too old.

2. It's really important we pick up the trash around school, guys. The school has become a dumping ground for our trash, and this needs to change. I think we should start being more respectful toward the school grounds and the custodian.

3. The student body would like you to add 15 minutes to the daily recess time since we believe it will directly improve our focus in the classroom. Physical fitness is just as important as academic achievement.

4. The local area is rundown and needs some new, entertaining places for teenagers. A youth center where teenagers can get together and participate in activities would improve the town.

5. I hope this message finds you well. I've spoken to a number of students around campus, and we feel that although your food is delicious, we would appreciate a healthier menu that incorporates more fruits and leafy greens.

6. I hope you are having a good day so far. I wanted to reach out and ask if it would be possible to work from 7 a.m. to 3 p.m. this Friday instead of my usual 9 a.m. to 5 p.m. My daughter has an appointment around 3:30 p.m. that day. Please let me know if this is possible at your earliest convenience. Thank you!

7. Stop going into my room when I'm not there! It's my private space with all of my belongings. You have your own room with your own things, which I don't go rummaging through.

Audiences

A. Principal

B. Boss

C. Local council

D. Sibling

E. Parents

F. School cook

G. Classmates

Lesson 2.3 Exercise: Who Is Your Audience?

Instructions: Now it's time to identify the audience of your essay. Work through the exercise by answering the questions.

The Audience

Who is your audience? _____
_____
_____

Formal or Informal

Does your writing need to be serious, or can it be more casual?
_____
_____

Tone

Will the reader understand complex words? _____
_____
_____

Will they understand technical terms?
_____
_____

Will they need definitions?
_____
_____

Audience's Background

Age? _____

Gender? _____

Interests? _____

Beliefs? _____

Education level? _____

Lesson 2.4: Brainstorming

When writing an essay, it's hard to know where to begin. Do you feel like you have nothing to write about? It can feel like there's an angry storm in your head, but this isn't what we mean by *brainstorming*.

Your brain is a muscle, and just like any other muscle in your body, it needs warming up. Brainstorming forces those rusty gears in your head to turn and takes the focus off writing, so your creative ideas can break free.

When you brainstorm, you come up with a whole heap of different ideas related to your prompt. You may not use them all, but this is how you get the big ideas that your essay will be based on (Arquilevich, 1999, p. 10).

There are plenty of methods used to brainstorm. We'll talk about two here:

1. Brainwriting
2. Idea Listing

 Study Skill: There are no rules when it comes to brainstorming. Go wild! Forget about trying to get your punctuation right or deciding whether an idea is silly. Everything connected to the prompt is worth writing down!

Brainwriting

This method is as simple as grabbing a piece of paper, putting your prompt in the middle, and writing as many ideas as you can that connect to it (Wilson et al., n.d.).

Using this method may help you get your ideas out quickly. You can scribble them down as they come to mind. This way, you won't forget any of your fantastic ideas. Take a look at the example.

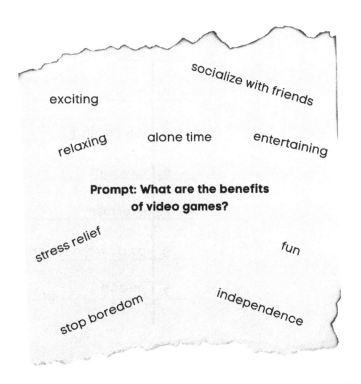

exciting

socialize with friends

relaxing   alone time   entertaining

Prompt: What are the benefits of video games?

stress relief   fun

stop boredom   independence

Idea Listing

If you like to keep your thoughts more organized, idea listing may be the best method for you (Purdue Writing Lab, n.d.-a).

It's an easy technique with just two steps:

1. Write your prompt at the top of the page.
2. List your ideas below your prompt.

Writing your prompt at the top of the page helps remind you of the focus of your essay, and it will bring you back on task if you get distracted. List your ideas in the order they come to mind.

This method may make it easier for you to pick out the main ideas you want to use in your essay later on.

	Prompt: How does nature help mental health?
1.	fresh air
2.	stress relief
3.	bright colors
4.	ecape
5.	interesting
6.	oxygen
7.	exercise
8.	away from technology
9.	peace

The Five Ws

What if no ideas immediately spring to mind? This happens all the time, so don't worry!

If you're finding it difficult knowing where to begin, try thinking about the five Ws:

1. Who?
2. What?
3. Where?
4. When?
5. Why?

Asking these questions in relation to your prompt may help you get started. But beware! You might find some questions don't relate to your prompt. That's OK! Just skip those and move onto one that sparks some ideas for you.

Take a look at the example. Use it as a guide when trying this method yourself!

Prompt: Describe the discovery of DNA.

What? Discovery of DNA

Who? Johann Friedrich Miescher

Where? In a laboratory in Tübingen castle. The room used to be a kitchen.

When? The 1860s

Why? To better understand the human body

Lesson 2.4 Exercise: Explosion of Ideas

Instructions: Let your ideas explode onto the page. Use this exercise when brainstorming to get those great ideas down. If you need some help, try filling in the 5 Ws on the next page.

Your Prompt:

Lesson 2.4 Exercise: The Five W's

Instructions: Fill in the 5 Ws if you need help or inspiration for the exercise on the previous page.

Your Prompt:

Who:

What:

Where:

When:

Why:

Lesson 2.4.1: Webbing

You have a whole load of ideas from your brainstorming, but this alone won't give you a great essay. To be able to make an essay plan out of your ideas, you need to connect them.

That's where webbing comes in. Webbing is a great way to connect your thoughts about your prompt. Just like a spider's web going from one surface to another, you draw lines between ideas that are related or similar in some way.

In a recent scientific study, 91.7% of students who took part said webbing would help them improve their writing. And in fact, it did (Ariana, 2015)! So, it's well worth giving it a go.

You may find that some ideas become grouped together because they are related, and you may notice a common thread between them. This is called *clustering*. Clustering is a great way to see what ideas are most important when it comes to your prompt.

Do some ideas have no connections at all? These are unlikely to be useful ideas when writing your essay (Arquilevich, 1999, p. 13). However, that doesn't mean get rid of them! Keep them, just in case.

Let's revisit the "how nature helps mental health" example we used when idea listing. Here, you can see it in web format!

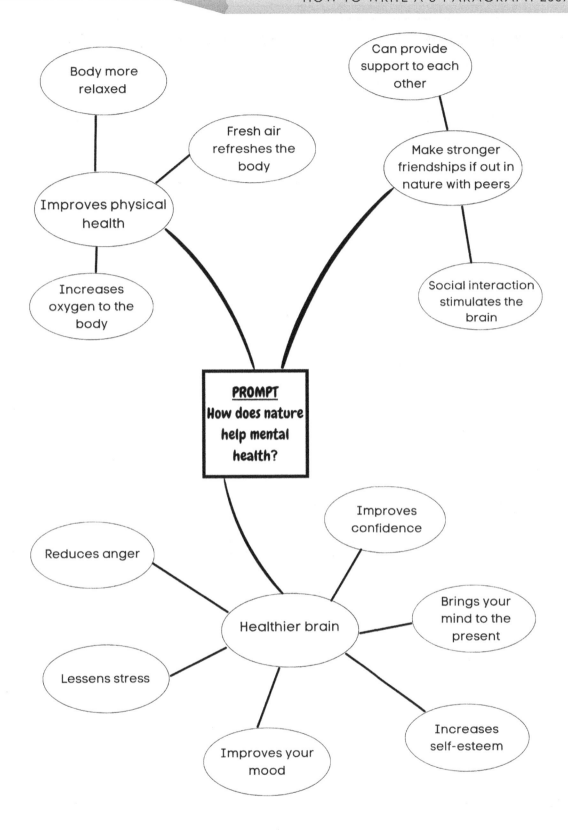

 Study Skill: Make a note along the line you draw about how one idea is connected to another, so you don't forget! You might find that multiple ideas are related to one another in clusters.

Lesson 2.4.1 Exercise: Webbing Your Way to a Great Essay

Instructions: Write your prompt in the middle square. Then, fill out the surrounding bubbles using ideas from your brainstorming session. Draw lines between any ideas that are related to one another. Do you notice any clustering?

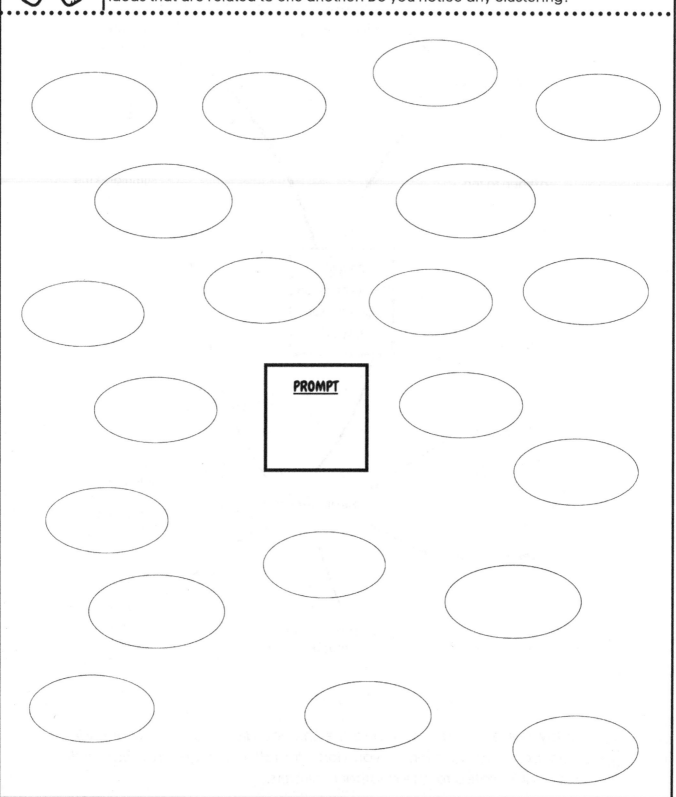

PROMPT

Lesson 2.5: Doing Your Research

If you picked your own prompt based on one of your interests, chances are you know some stuff about it already. If your teacher chose it for you, however, you may know very little about it.

Whatever the situation, researching is a great tool to improve your knowledge of your essay subject. This makes writing your essay a lot easier!

Researching for essay writing is important for many reasons:

- Your brain will be overflowing with knowledge, which will show in your essay.
- Knowing more about your topic will give your writing clarity.
- You'll find interesting facts about your topic that not everyone knows, which will make your essay more exciting to read.
- Your essay will be based on fact, not fiction.
- When you have lots of information, you can pick out the best parts, which makes your essay more creative and effective.

As you can see, we could go on forever about the benefits of research. But there are some important things to think about when finding information.

Some sources are better than others. For example, you can't use information your mom's friend's nephew said about your prompt, but you *can* interview an expert.

The easiest place to find information in a short amount of time is the internet. But beware! Not all the information you see there is factual or relevant to your prompt.

Books are a great way to find trustworthy information. Take a look at different dictionaries. Perhaps there's an encyclopedia on your essay subject (Arquilevich, 1999, pp. 15–16)!

Study Skill: Check through a book's index for keywords, so you can quickly skip through pages that have nothing to do with your prompt—this will save you a lot of time!

There are two worries students typically have when it comes to research:

1. How to know what is fact and what is not
2. What to research

Let's go through these in a bit more detail.

Separating Truth from Lies

There are some things you can do to make sure your sources are reliable. Here are some tips to help you out:

1. Check out the author or publisher. Do a quick internet search for them. Find their experience and education to be sure they're an expert on your essay subject.
2. Ask yourself: Why is the author writing this information? Is it to help people learn about the subject? Are they trying to be funny or over-the-top? Are they trying to sell something?
3. Look at plenty of sources. If they all say the same thing, you can probably trust them.
4. Check the date. If you're talking about a historical event in your essay, information may be more trustworthy if it's from that particular time period. If you're focusing on a more modern subject, you may want to stick to more current sources so the information is still relevant.
5. Avoid social media posts, advertisements, and blogs, as these aren't usually reliable sources.

What Do I Research?

If you're asking yourself, "What do I research?" don't worry! This is why we brainstorming and webbing. You're already prepared for this.

Go back to your brainstorm and webbing sheets. Take some keywords from these and use them in your research.

Save Your Sources!

The last thing to remember is to write down your sources as you find them. Showing where you got your information is an important part of essay writing.

It's so common for students to do brilliant research, then close the tab (or close the book) and lose the source forever. What a waste of time!

It's a lot harder trying to go back to find your sources once you've written your essay, so do it as you go along! It's critical to give credit to those whose information you used (Arquilevich, 1999, pp. 15–16).

Lesson 2.5 Exercise: Saving Your Sources

Instructions: When you come across a source while researching, write it down here so that you don't lose it. Remember to check that it's reliable using the five tips in Lesson 2.5. Can you write down what makes your sources trustworthy?

Example

Prompt: What are the positives and negatives of being a serious athlete? Explain your answer.

Book Source
- Book Title: <u>The Trial of Miles: A Disabled Runner's Memoir</u>
- Author: Cort Schneider
- Copyright Date: 2019
- Page(s): 50

Why is it trustworthy?
Cort Schneider has personal experience as a serious athlete and has adapted to living with cerebral palsy.

Internet Source
https://nutritionfacts.org/2022/03/10/water-vs-coconut-water-vs-sports-drinks-for-athletes/

Why is it trustworthy?
Michael Greger, the author, is a physician and an authority within the realm of nutrition. In this article, he provides his expertise and cites several studies from the National Library of Medicine.

Interview Source
Name: LeBron James
Date: September 17, 2021

Why is it trustworthy?
He is a professional athlete.

Your turn! Record your sources on the next page.

Lesson 2.5 Exercise: Saving Your Sources

Instructions: When you come across a source while researching, write it down here so that you don't lose it. Remember to check that it's reliable using the five tips in Lesson 2.5. Can you write down what makes your sources trustworthy?

Source 1: _____

_____

_____

_____

Source 2: _____

_____

_____

_____

Source 3: _____

_____

_____

_____

Source 4: _____

_____

_____

_____

Source 5: _____

_____

_____

_____

Source 6: _____

_____

_____

_____

Lesson 2.6: Stating Your Claim

Now that you have your research and sources all sorted out, we're going to explore *stating your claim*, an imperative step in the essay planning process. Let's get started with what a claim actually is.

Claim: a statement that establishes the main idea or argument of your essay (The Writing Center @PVCC, 2017).

In other words, a claim is usually a sentence that conveys a point of view or opinion on which an essay is based (Matthews, 2020, p. 13). It determines the essay's goal and direction. The claim is always supported by evidence.

When we talk about *evidence*, we mean those trustworthy sources you found in your research. These sources are going to be your best friend when it comes to the next lesson, Backing Up Your Claim.

Say your prompt is: "What is the most popular animal in America?" During your research, you found reliable sources saying dogs are the most common pet and evidence proving this. Using these sources to back it up, you can claim that dogs are the most popular animal in America.

How to Come Up with a Claim

For starters, your claim needs to be related to your essay prompt. It should be a statement, not an instruction or a question (Matthews, 2020, p. 13).

Here's an example to help you out:

Prompt: Describe the difficulties of getting good grades.

Claim: Getting good grades is difficult.

Remember earlier how we spoke about subject words? If you've forgotten, these are the words in your prompt that tell you what you need to write about. These aren't always one or two words; they can also be a phrase.

As well as helping you understand your prompt, subject words can also help you generate your claim!

If we're using the example above, the subject words would be "difficulties of getting good grades."

Can you see what we've done to make the claim? We've taken the subject words and created a statement that can be proven.

Let's do another one:

Prompt: What is the most successful NFL team?

Subject Words: most successful NFL team

Claim: The most successful NFL team is the New England Patriots.

What if You Have a Clashing Phrase in Your Prompt?

You might be wondering how you would state a claim for a prompt that contains a clashing phrase. This might seem confusing, but have no fear! Let's break it down.

When a prompt contains a clashing phrase, it's asking you for *two* sides of an argument, like "for **and** against" or "advantages **and** disadvantages." However, when it comes to your claim, you will only choose *one* side. The *other* side will come into play when you gather evidence for your claim in the next lesson.

If your prompt is "discuss the pros and cons of watching the news," your claim could be "watching the news has an overall negative effect on your brain." Notice here your claim only makes *one* finite argument. You're arguing the news is bad for your brain (cons) based on the research you've done and the sources you found.

Even though the pros of watching the news is not reflected in your claim, don't forget it's of great importance later on. It will make more sense in Lesson 2.7, as you keep moving forward in this chapter.

Let's go through an example:

Prompt: What are the advantages **and** disadvantages of taking vitamin supplements?

Subject Words: advantages and disadvantages of taking vitamin supplements

Claim: Overall, taking vitamin supplements is good for you.

In this example, we took the side of advantages in our claim.

Note: You can get creative with your claim. It doesn't have to include the same exact wording as your subject words.

Now that we've covered all the bases, you're ready to try it out for yourself with your prompt!

Lesson 2.6 Exercise: Essay Prompt → Subject Words → Claim

Instructions: Work through the exercise starting at the essay prompt. Pick out the subject words and create a claim using these keywords. Use the example as a guide.

Example:

Prompt:
What are the effects of eating fast food every day?

→

Subject Words:
the effects of eating fast food every day

→

Claim:
Eating fast food every day is detrimental to your health.

---

① **Prompt:**
Describe the negative impact of texting while driving.

→

Subject Words:

→

Claim:

---

② **Prompt:**
What are the effects of weather on mood? Analyze the pros and cons.

→

Subject Words:

→

Claim:

---

③ **Prompt:**
Does the color of someone's bedroom walls affect their mental health?

→

Subject Words:

→

Claim:

Lesson 2.6 Exercise: Essay Prompt → Subject Words → Claim

Instructions: Work through the exercise starting at the essay prompt. Pick out the subject words and create a claim using these keywords. Use the example as a guide.

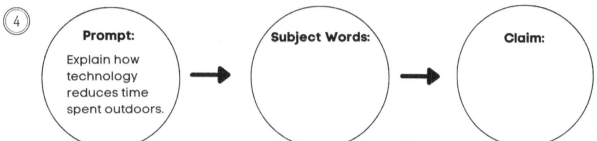

④ **Prompt:** Explain how technology reduces time spent outdoors.

Subject Words:

Claim:

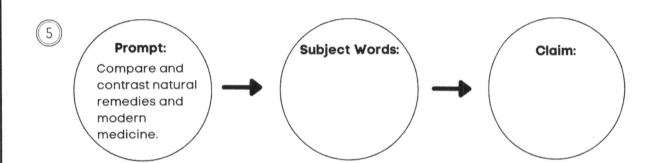

⑤ **Prompt:** Compare and contrast natural remedies and modern medicine.

Subject Words:

Claim:

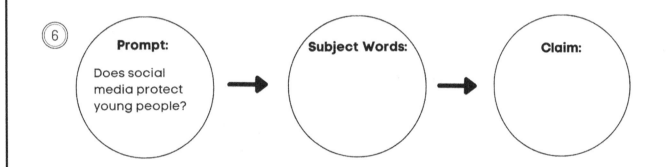

⑥ **Prompt:** Does social media protect young people?

Subject Words:

Claim:

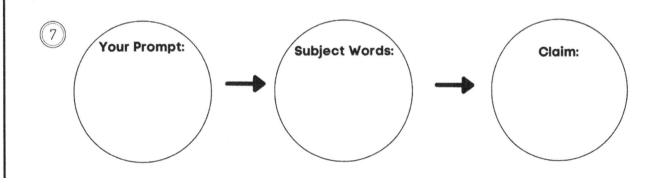

⑦ **Your Prompt:**

Subject Words:

Claim:

Lesson 2.7: Backing Up Your Claim

Unfortunately, just stating your claim isn't enough. After all, if a friend told you it's going to rain candy tomorrow, you wouldn't believe them unless they could show evidence, right?

So, that's what you need—evidence for your claim. This is called *backing up your claim*, and it's where your research comes in handy.

What Are Supporting Points?

Supporting points are the *key reasons* you use to back up your claim.

They show your reader *why* you believe in your claim and demonstrate why the reader should believe it, too!

Supporting points need to directly relate to your claim or else they won't back it up (Matthews, 2020, pp. 15–16). Let's take a look at this example:

Prompt: Are interpersonal skills important when building a career? Explain your answer.

Claim: Interpersonal skills are important when building a career.

Supporting Point: more likely to get a job

What makes this a supporting point?

- It directly relates to the claim.
- It explains why the claim is true.

Rule of Three

You may have noticed things often come in threes, especially in writing. Have you heard the common saying, "blood, sweat, and tears"? Maybe that's what you felt you were putting into your essay writing before!

Presenting things in threes, like in the phrase above, is called the *rule of three*.

Put simply, we use threes because our brain finds this easier to process and remember. This is because it forms a pattern. In fact, it forms the smallest pattern possible, which is why our brains like it so much (Gigasavvy, 2014). It's easy to remember!

Why are we bringing this up now? Well, when you're coming up with your supporting points, it's important to remember the rule of three.

Rule of Three and Supporting Points

Using the rule of three in your essay will make the difference between a good five-paragraph essay and a great one.

One way to bring the rule of three into your essay is through your supporting points. Giving the reader not one, not two, but three supporting points will really showcase *why* you believe in the claim you're making.

Let's add two more supporting points to the previous example to fully back up the claim:

Prompt: Are interpersonal skills important when building a career? Explain your answer.

Claim: Interpersonal skills are important when building a career.

Supporting Point 1: more likely to get a job

Supporting Point 2: reduces stress

Supporting Point 3: makes you better at working in a team

Opposing Points

So, we've talked about supporting points, but what about opposing ones?

Opposing points are *reasons* that argue *against* your claim. In other words, they offer the counterargument, which is important to show you are capable of understanding and addressing multiple opinions. Now, **not all essays will need opposing points**, so how do you tell?

You can often tell if you need opposing points when there is a clashing phrase within the prompt. Remember, we previously discussed clashing phrases in Lesson 2.2. To jog your memory, here's the list again:

- Advantages **and** disadvantages
- Positives **and** negatives
- Pros **and** cons
- Compare **and** contrast
- Benefits **and** drawbacks
- For **and** against
- Similarities **and** differences

*Study Skill: Look for a clashing phrase with **and** in your prompt. This usually indicates the need for an opposing point. If it is **or** instead of **and**, you do not need an opposing point.*

Recall the words in these clashing phrases oppose or *clash* with one another by asking you for **different** things. Though your claim is a single argument, as discussed in Lesson 2.6, you may need to make points that support your claim and also a point that opposes your claim. So, when you see a clashing phrase, recognize you will need both supporting points and *an* opposing point (Matthews, 2020, p. 15).

The rule of three still applies when including opposing points in your essay.

It may look like this:

Prompt: Discuss reasons for and against the following statement: Interpersonal skills are important when building a career.

Claim: Interpersonal skills are important when building a career.

Supporting Point 1: more likely to get a job

Supporting Point 2: reduces stress

Opposing Point: interpersonal skills not important for some jobs

Two supporting points and one opposing point

Lesson 2.7 Exercise: Backing Up Your Claim

Instructions: Use the word bank to match the supporting and opposing points with the correct claim! Use your own claim and come up with supporting points for your essay. Remember to come up with an opposing point if necessary!

It causes lung damage.

Vegetables contain lots of vitamins and minerals.

Fall is apple picking season.

A vegetarian diet typically has fewer calories.

It makes the immune system weaker.

Vitamin B12 is more readily available in a meat diet than in a meat-free diet.

The leaves on trees change color.

Everything comes in pumpkin spice flavor.

It increases the risk of blood clots.

---

1. **Prompt:** Describe the effects of smoking on the body.

What is the claim? Smoking is bad for your health.

Supporting Point 1: _____

Supporting Point 2: _____

Supporting Point 3: _____

(Centers for Disease Control and Prevention [CDC], 2021b)

2. **Prompt:** What is the best season? Explain your answer.

What is the claim? Fall is the best season.

Supporting Point 1: _____

Supporting Point 2: _____

Supporting Point 3: _____

3. **Prompt:** Is a meat-free diet good for you? Analyze the pros **and** cons.

What is the claim? A meat-free diet is good for you.

Supporting Point 1: _____

Supporting Point 2: _____

Opposing Point:
_____

Lesson 2.7 Exercise: Backing Up Your Claim

Instructions: Use the word bank to match the supporting and opposing points with the correct claim! Use your own claim and come up with supporting points for your essay. Remember to come up with an opposing point if necessary!

It increases memory capacity.

It creates habit and strengthens talent.

It reduces loneliness.

Practicing a skill helps learning.

It improves communication skills.

It helps store information in long-term memory.

---

4. **Prompt:** Do you agree **or** disagree with the phrase "practice makes perfect"?

What is the claim? Practice does make perfect.

Supporting Point 1: _____

Supporting Point 2: _____

Supporting Point 3: _____

5. **Prompt:** Discuss the benefits of socializing with friends.

What is the claim? Socializing with friends is good for you.

Supporting Point 1: _____

Supporting Point 2: _____

Supporting Point 3: _____

6. **Your prompt:** _____

What is your claim? _____

Supporting Point 1: _____

Supporting Point 2: _____

Supporting Point 3: _____
(or Opposing Point)

Lesson 2.7 Exercise: Supports, Opposes, or Not Relevant?

Instructions: Here, you have points paired with a claim. Decide whether each point supports the claim, opposes the claim, or isn't relevant at all to the claim! Circle the best answer.

1. **Prompt:** Describe the spread of false information.

Claim: False information is spread through social media.

Point: Social media shares a lot of "fake news."

A. Supports

B. Opposes

C. Not relevant

2. **Prompt:** Explain the positives of sleep.

Claim: Sleep is good for you because it improves your health.

Point: Too much sleep can make your body feel lousy and tired the next day.

A. Supports

B. Opposes

C. Not relevant

3. **Prompt:** Discuss the similarities and differences between hot dogs and hamburgers.

Claim: Hot dogs and hamburgers are similar.

Point: Steak is cooked in the same way as hot dogs and hamburgers.

A. Supports

B. Opposes

C. Not relevant

4. **Prompt:** Explain what makes someone a bully.

Claim: A bully is someone who repeatedly harms another person.

Point: A bully doesn't harm others.

A. Supports

B. Opposes

C. Not relevant

Lesson 2.7 Exercise: Supports, Opposes, or Not Relevant?

Instructions: Here, you have points paired with a claim. Decide whether each point supports the claim, opposes the claim, or isn't relevant at all to the claim! Circle the best answer.

5. **Prompt:** Compare and contrast high school and college.

Claim: High school and college are similar.

Point: They both have a summer break.

A. Supports

B. Opposes

C. Not relevant

6. **Prompt:** Explain the similarities and differences between bacteria and viruses.

Claim: Bacteria and viruses are very different.

Point: Most bacteria are harmless, but most viruses cause infections.

A. Supports

B. Opposes

C. Not relevant

7. **Prompt:** Is American football the most popular sport in America?

Claim: American football is not the most popular sport in America.

Point: It receives more live views than other sports.

A. Supports

B. Opposes

C. Not relevant

8. **Prompt:** What is more popular, television or video games? Explain your answer.

Claim: Television is more popular than video games.

Point: Video games bring in more money than music (Czajka, 2020).

A. Supports

B. Opposes

C. Not relevant

Lesson 2.8: Coming Up with a Killer Thesis Statement

You may be sitting there wondering what on Earth a thesis statement is. We have you covered!

Thesis statement: a sentence that brings together the central ideas of your essay

You'll include your thesis statement at the end of your first paragraph, the introduction. It's an essential part of your essay because it shows the audience your main ideas and the order you will present them in your essay.

A good thesis statement is

- specific,
- clear, and
- concise.

Your thesis statement needs to be specific to your prompt. Otherwise, it'll confuse the reader. If it's not specific, they won't know what your essay is really about!

It needs to present a clear argument for the same reason. You want the reader to think, *OK, this is what the essay is arguing for!*

Making your thesis statement concise stops the reader from getting bored. Use clear, simple language to keep them interested.

How Do You Do It?

For a thesis statement, we will combine the parts you've worked on so far. That's your claim and your three points. Add these together in a simple sentence, and voila! You have your thesis statement (Matthews, 2020, p. 22).

Let's look at an example.

Essay prompt: Why is going to school important?

Claim: Going to school is important.

Supporting Point 1: to get an education

Supporting Point 2: to make life-long friends

Supporting Point 3: to gain social skills

Thesis Statement: Going to school is important because it allows you to get an education, to make lifelong friends, and to gain social skills.

If you need more clarification, here's another example:

Essay prompt: Explain why potato chips make the perfect snack.

Claim: Potato chips make the perfect snack.

Supporting Point 1: They're crunchy.

Supporting Point 2: They're satisfyingly salty.

Supporting Point 3: They come in many flavors.

Thesis Statement: Potato chips make the perfect snack because they're crunchy, they're satisfyingly salty, and they come in many flavors.

If you include both *supporting points* **and** *opposing points* in your thesis statement, you have multiple options for how you can write it. The formula for your thesis in these cases is not complicated. You will most likely include words similar to these:

- Despite
- In spite of
- Whereas
- Even though
- However
- Although
- But
- Yet

If you're still stuck, check out the example.

- **Prompt:** "Bananas are one of the best fruits." Argue for **and** against this statement.
- **Claim:** Bananas are one of the best fruits.

- **Supporting Point 1:** They contain vitamins.
- **Supporting Point 2:** They are generally inexpensive.
- **Opposing Point:** They contain little protein.
- **Thesis Statement:** Bananas contain little protein, but their high vitamin content and their low cost make them one of the best fruits.

However, you don't have to stick to that exact sentence structure. You can use other words to help you convey your argument! Take a look at how we've adapted the thesis statement for this prompt.

- **Option 2:** Despite bananas containing little protein, they are inexpensive and rich in vitamins, making them one of the best fruits.
- **Option 3:** Although bananas contain little protein, because of their vitamin content and low cost, they're still one of the best fruits.
- **Option 4:** Bananas are one of the best fruits because of their vitamin content and low cost, which make up for their low protein levels.
- **Option 5:** Even though bananas contain less protein than some other fruits, their vitamin content and low cost make up for this disadvantage, so they're still one of the best fruits.
- **Option 6:** Although bananas contain little protein, they are one of the best fruits because they are generally inexpensive and contain vitamins.

See, there are so many ways to write a thesis statement when you have an opposing point! Choose which way works best for you. Get creative!

Lesson 2.8 Exercise: Practicing Thesis Statements

Instructions: Combine the claims and supporting/opposing points together to form thesis statements. Try writing your own thesis statement for the last one.

① **Prompt:** Do some people work harder than others? Explain your reasoning.

Claim: Some people work harder than others.

Supporting Point 1: motivation to reach the top of the ladder

Supporting Point 2: have to provide for others (e.g., their children)

Supporting Point 3: more positive attitude toward work

Thesis Statement: _____

_____

_____

② **Prompt:** Discuss the positives of taking a gap year to travel after college.

Claim: Students should take a gap year after college.

Supporting Point 1: It increases self-awareness.

Supporting Point 2: It boosts confidence and improves communication skills.

Supporting Point 3: It helps develop an understanding of other cultures.

Thesis Statement:

_____

_____

Prompt: Should grades be replaced with a pass/fail system?

③ **Claim:** Grades should be replaced with pass/fail.

Supporting Point 1: less stress for the students

Supporting Point 2: less competition between classmates

Opposing Point: lower motivation without grades

Thesis Statement:

_____

_____

_____

Lesson 2.8 Exercise: Practicing Thesis Statements

Instructions: Combine the claims and supporting/opposing points together to form thesis statements. Try writing your own thesis statement for the last one.

④ **Prompt:** What are the most important life skills?

Claim: There are several life skills more important than all others.

Supporting Point 1: communication skills for building relationships

Supporting Point 2: problem-solving skills for tough situations

Supporting Point 3: self-awareness to grow as an individual

Thesis Statement: _____

_____

_____

⑤ **Prompt:** Discuss the differences between mammals and reptiles.

Claim: There are many differences between mammals and reptiles.

Supporting Point 1: Mammals have hair, and reptiles usually have scales (Study.com, 2022).

Supporting Point 2: Mammals have four-chambered hearts, and reptiles have three-chambered hearts.

Supporting Point 3: Reptiles lay eggs, and mammals have live births.

Thesis Statement: _____

_____

_____

⑥ **Prompt:** _____

Claim: _____

Supporting Point 1: _____

Supporting Point 2: _____

Supporting Point 3/Opposing Point: _____

_____

Thesis Statement: _____

_____

*Keep this safe, as it's going to be a big help when you start your outline in Chapter 3!

Chapter 2 Comprehension Quiz

Instructions: Circle the best answer.

1. **What are the two most common problems people have with picking topics?**
   a. The topic isn't interesting.
   b. The topic is too big.
   c. The topic is too informal.
   d. Both A and C

2. **After you've come up with your topic, what is the next step?**
   a. Transform it into a thesis statement.
   b. Transform it into an introduction paragraph.
   c. Transform it into an outline.
   d. Transform it into a prompt.

3. **What are subject words?**
   a. Words that tell you how to write your introduction
   b. Words that tell you what you need to write about
   c. Words that tell you what you need to do
   d. Words that tell you how to write your outline

4. **What are command words?**
   a. Words that tell you what you need to do
   b. Words that tell you how to write your introduction
   c. Words that tell you what you need to write about
   d. Words that tell you how to write your outline

5. **What is "webbing"?**
   a. A method used to come up with topic ideas
   b. A technique used to transform your topic into a prompt
   c. A method used to write your introduction
   d. A technique used to connect the ideas from your brainstorm

Instructions: Circle the best answer.

6. **Why is researching important?**
   a. Your essay will be based on reliable information.
   b. You learn about irrelevant topics.
   c. Your writing will be clearer.
   d. A and C

7. **How can you check if your source is reliable?**
   a. Check the date.
   b. Check multiple sources.
   c. Check the author.
   d. All of the above

8. **What is a claim?**
   a. A statement you come up with at the end of your essay
   b. A statement that isn't related to your prompt
   c. A statement that establishes the main idea or argument of your essay
   d. Your title

9. **What are the statements that you use to support your claim?**
   a. Opposing points
   b. Supporting points
   c. A title
   d. A topic

10. **How do you form a thesis statement?**
    a. Combine the topic with your prompt.
    b. Combine your prompt with your claim.
    c. Combine your claim with your introduction.
    d. Combine your claim with your three points (could be three supporting or two supporting and one opposing point).

CHAPTER 3

Outlining Your Way to Success

You've successfully completed the first part of the Prewriting step. Now, onto the next! This chapter is all about *outlining* and covers these lessons:

3.1.   Formal Outline
3.2.   The Handy Hamburger
3.3.   Mind Maps
3.4.   Timeline Graphic Organizer
3.5.   Flowchart

A sense of dread can begin to creep in at this point, knowing this is the last step before actually writing your essay. You might feel a bit lost, like you don't know where to go next.

Don't be afraid. Your outline is a guide that will point you in the right direction.

In this chapter, we'll teach you different outlining techniques. That way, if one doesn't work for you, just pick a different one!

We'll go over the more traditional outlining technique first. Then, we'll explore some graphic organizer methods, which aren't as formal but are a lot of fun, especially for visual learners!

 Study Skill: You don't need to be an artist or designer to make a great graphic organizer. The most important part is being thoughtful about your ideas.

What is an Outline, Anyway?

Outlines are a way for you to organize your thoughts before you begin writing. They map out your entire essay. By looking at your outline, you'll know the following:

- What to say in your introduction
- What each paragraph is going to be about
- How you're going to move from one paragraph to the next
- The points you want to make to wrap up your essay

You need a prompt, a claim, three supporting points (an opposing point if applicable), and a thesis statement for your outline. Would you look at that? You already have those!

What Is the Purpose?

When you're overwhelmed by the task of writing your essay, it's easy to come to the outline and think, *What's the point?*

Well, a muddled head leads to a messy essay! Skipping this process means your essay will most probably be unorganized and contain unnecessary information that's unrelated to your prompt. It may also dart from one idea to another without any real structure.

And if all that isn't bad enough, teachers can tell! They look for whether an essay is organized or not.

There's a whole host of benefits to outlining:

- A good outline = less time spent writing your essay.
- Better focus on the task at hand, rather than going off-course.
- Your transitions between paragraphs will be smoother, giving your essay better flow.
- You will avoid unnecessary rambling, making your writing clearer and more concise (Kittelstad, n.d.).

Now can you see why outlining is so essential?

Why Use Graphic Organizers?

Graphic organizers work in the same way as traditional outlines: They organize your ideas so you can present a well-thought-out and cohesive essay. They're visual displays that bring together facts and ideas about a prompt. In this case, your essay prompt!

You may have only used traditional outline methods up to this point. Why bother with something new? Well, graphic organizers

- simplify information, so it's easy to understand,
- make complex content fun and interactive,
- trigger past knowledge you may not even realize you have,
- improve concentration and understanding, and
- get your brain working hard through visual prompts (Network Support, n.d.).

If the thought of staring at a blank page terrifies you, graphic organizers are here to help! With instructions to follow, you'll finally know where to start and which direction to go in.

But first, let's look at a formal outlining method.

Different Types of Outlining Methods

Lesson 3.1: Formal Outline

Creating Your Outline!

Your essay outline doesn't have to be long. It's just a place where you can summarize your main points. You can refer back to it while you're writing. That way, you'll stay on track!

You'll need the following for your outline:

- Prompt
- Claim
- Thesis statement
- Supporting points (with possible opposing point)

So, here's the *basic* flow of an outline:

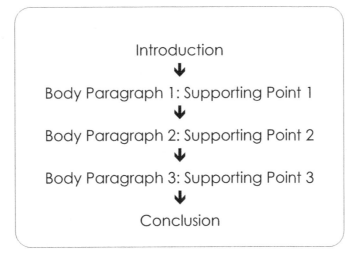

This is the order in which your outline will be presented. The introduction section is where your killer thesis statement goes. Remember, your thesis statement is made up of your *claim* and supporting points (with possible opposing point) put together.

For the supporting point sections in your outline, you'll need to write your supporting points. Each supporting point corresponds with one of the *three* body paragraphs in your five-paragraph essay.

Put some thought into how each supporting point relates to your claim. How does it reinforce and *support* your claim? *Why* is your supporting point important or true?

In your outline, you will consider these thoughts and briefly bullet point any ideas that come to mind in the supporting point sections. The research you've previously done should help you here. This part of the outline is crucial to setting you up for success when you write your body paragraphs, but try not to stress about how many bullet points you are adding. You may have one in-depth bullet point you want to talk about or three you think are worth discussing. As you develop your thoughts in the later lessons, you will have a better sense of what works best for proving your thesis.

If your prompt contains a clashing phrase, remember instead of having three supporting points, you need **two** *supporting* points and **one** *opposing* point. Swap Supporting Point 3 out and replace it with your opposing point, like in the example!

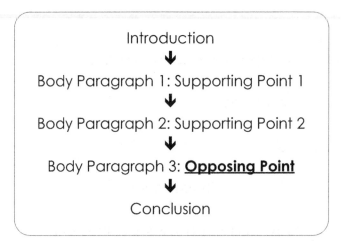

Introduction
↓
Body Paragraph 1: Supporting Point 1
↓
Body Paragraph 2: Supporting Point 2
↓
Body Paragraph 3: **Opposing Point**
↓
Conclusion

You will still consider how your opposing point *relates* to your claim. However, clearly your opposing point does not *support* your claim. Rather, it acts as a counterargument that refutes your claim.

You must think about why your claim still holds true despite your opposing point. Think about why your opposing point is not a big deal. Why is your opposing point not an issue? Consider why it isn't important.

Again, briefly bullet point any ideas that come to mind in the opposing point section, which would correspond with Body Paragraph 3.

The last step is the conclusion. Here, you simply rephrase your thesis statement for the purpose of the outline. You can use more than one sentence if necessary. New information and ideas are not appropriate in this section, so don't add anything extra. The conclusion is supposed to tie your essay together.

Let's check out an example of a formal outline:

Prompt: What are the benefits of a good night's sleep?
Claim: A good night's sleep is beneficial.

Introduction → Thesis Statement: A good night's sleep is beneficial because it boosts your emotional health, reduces your chance of getting ill, and keeps you at a healthy weight.

Body Paragraph 1 → Supporting Point 1: A good night's sleep boosts your emotional health.
• Sleep makes you feel happy and energized when you wake up in the morning.
• You'll feel grateful and ready to conquer the day.
• You'll be fresh-faced and feel more confident about yourself.

*Think about how having a good night's sleep boosts emotional health. How does this supporting point reinforce the claim?

Body Paragraph 2 → Supporting Point 2: A good night's sleep reduces your chance of getting ill.
• Immune system will have a chance to reset and recover while you sleep
• Body can fight off infection while you sleep instead of expending energy elsewhere
• Giving muscles an opportunity to rest reduces chance of getting ill

*Think about how having a good night's sleep reduces the chance of getting ill. How does this supporting point reinforce the claim?

Body Paragraph 3 → Supporting Point 3: A good night's sleep keeps you at a healthy weight.
• Helps you stay away from midnight snacking and gaining weight
• Keeps you energized enough to be physically active and maintain a healthy weight
• Keeps your metabolism balanced

*Think about how having a good night's sleep keeps you at a healthy weight. How does this supporting point reinforce the claim?

Conclusion → Rephrased Thesis Statement: Although staying up late can be fun, it's important to note sufficient sleep at night is important for good emotional health and avoiding sickness. In many cases, it helps you maintain a healthy weight as well.

If your third body paragraph includes an opposing point and not a supporting point, here's what that section in your outline would look like instead:

Body Paragraph 3 → Opposing Point: A good night's sleep can be bad for you when you overdo it (Osmun, 2022).
• Too much sleep is linked to increased risk of chronic diseases in adults over the age of 45.
• Too much sleep can be an indication of depression in individuals.
• Too much sleep and sleeping in is often linked to higher rates of headaches.

*Think about how this opposing point isn't a big deal. Despite this opposing point, why is your claim still true?

If you're all done here, let's crack on with your outline!

Lesson 3.1 Exercise: Formal Essay Outline

Instructions: Work through the exercise, filling out each section, to create your essay outline. The example in Lesson 3.1 is there to help you!

Prompt: _____
Claim: _____

Introduction → Thesis Statement: _____
_____
_____
_____

Body Paragraph 1 → Supporting Point 1: _____
_____
_____
_____

*Think about how this supporting point reinforces the claim.

Body Paragraph 2 → Supporting Point 2: _____
_____
_____
_____

*Think about how this supporting point reinforces the claim.

Body Paragraph 3 → Supporting Point 3 OR Opposing Point: ____
_____
_____
_____

*Think about how this supporting point reinforces the claim OR why your claim is still true despite this opposing point.

Conclusion → Rephrased Thesis Statement: _____
_____
_____
_____

Lesson 3.2: The Handy Hamburger

The five-paragraph essay has another name—maybe you've heard it before? It's called the "hamburger" essay. You might not like essays as much as you like hamburgers, but you're about to!

Why the Name?

Well, you know there are different parts to a hamburger. You have the bottom bun, the mouth-watering fillings in the middle (like the meat, tomato, and lettuce), and then the top bun. Each part of the hamburger represents a paragraph in your five-paragraph essay.

The top bun is your introduction. It's the thing you taste first. The bottom bun is your conclusion. Together, they hold the meat, tomato, and lettuce in place. If we didn't have the bun, the best bits would fall out all over the place. Your introduction and conclusion work in the same way. They hold the goodies, your supporting/opposing points, together. And remember, each point corresponds with one of the three body paragraphs.

Each part is essential. No one wants a burger with no bun, and who wants a burger with no delicious filling?

 Study Skill: If hamburgers aren't your thing, there are some other analogies that might work for you. What about sleeping in a bed? The blanket is the introduction, you are the body paragraphs, and the bed is the conclusion.

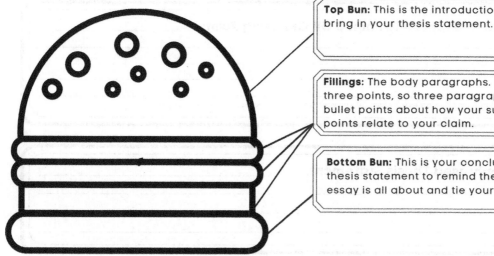

Top Bun: This is the introduction. This is where you bring in your thesis statement.

Fillings: The body paragraphs. Remember, you have three points, so three paragraphs! Don't forget the bullet points about how your supporting/opposing points relate to your claim.

Bottom Bun: This is your conclusion. Rephrase your thesis statement to remind the reader what your essay is all about and tie your essay together.

Lesson 3.2 Exercise: The Handy Hamburger Outline

Instructions: Work through each section of the Handy Hamburger. Look at the example in Lesson 3.1 (formal outline) if you need help. This outline follows the same structure.

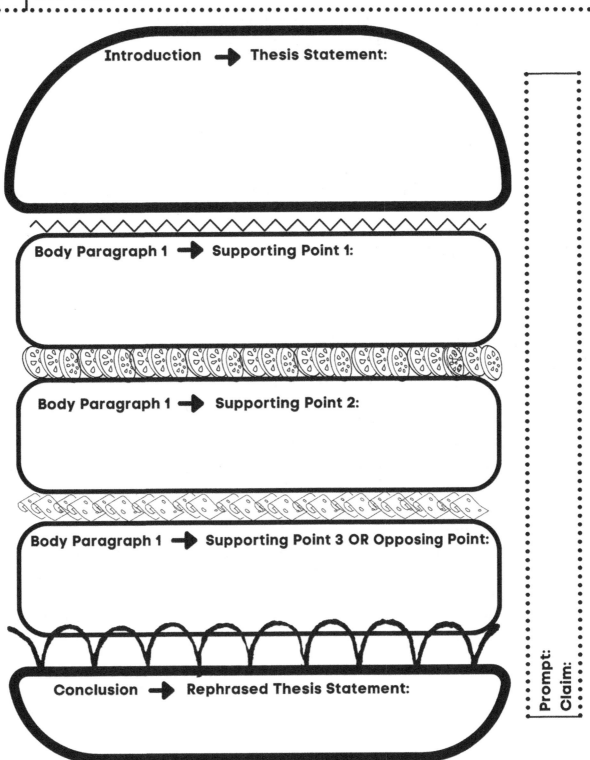

Introduction ➡ **Thesis Statement:**

Body Paragraph 1 ➡ **Supporting Point 1:**

Body Paragraph 1 ➡ **Supporting Point 2:**

Body Paragraph 1 ➡ **Supporting Point 3 OR Opposing Point:**

Conclusion ➡ **Rephrased Thesis Statement:**

Prompt:
Claim:

Lesson 3.3: Mind Maps

Mind maps are a useful tool because they can make a dull task a bit more fun and save you a lot of time!

A mind map is a visual diagram. It tends to have the prompt in the center with lots of lines (or "branches") connecting to bubbles around it.

Mind maps have been scientifically proven to do the following:

- Improve essay structure
- Make essay writing clearer (Holland et al., 2003)
- Improve memory of factual information (Farrand et al., 2002)
- Increase motivation and enjoyment while learning (Goodnough & Woods, 2002)

How Do You Do It?

To make a mind map, follow six simple steps:

1. Write your essay prompt in the center of your page.
2. Draw five branches going from your essay prompt to the empty spaces on your page. You'll want to start off with five branches, one for each of the five paragraphs: Introduction, Body Paragraph 1, Body Paragraph 2, Body Paragraph 3, and Conclusion. Label all five branches (aka paragraphs) at the end of the line you've drawn. Then, draw a bubble around the paragraph names.
3. Draw branches coming off the bubbles you created. These branches will be for all the information related to the five paragraphs.
4. For the introduction, you'll need to draw a branch coming off of it for your thesis statement.
5. Draw a branch coming off of each body paragraph for your supporting (or opposing) point. Then, draw branches coming off of your supporting (or opposing) point for those bullet points we talked about in Lesson 3.1!
6. Lastly, draw a branch coming off of your conclusion for rephrasing the thesis statement.

Let's look at an example with this prompt to give you a clear visual: Explain how mind maps improve learning.

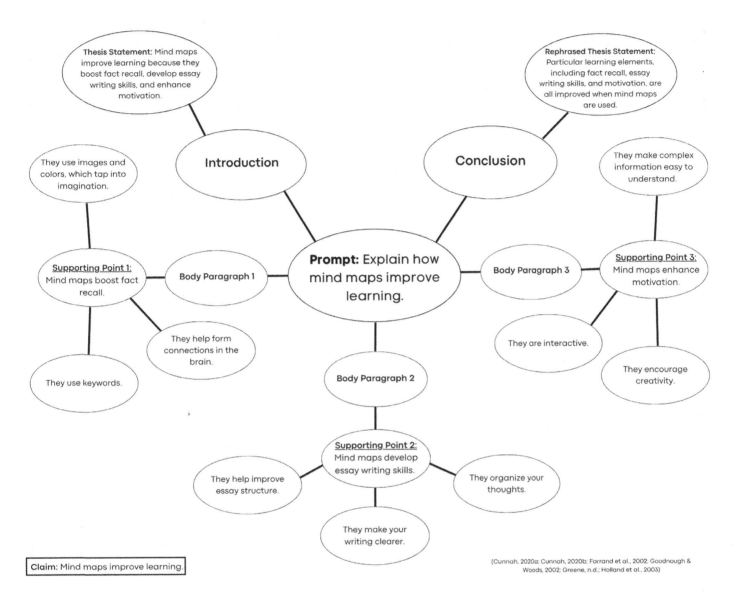

Thesis Statement: Mind maps improve learning because they boost fact recall, develop essay writing skills, and enhance motivation.

Introduction

They use images and colors, which tap into imagination.

Supporting Point 1: Mind maps boost fact recall.

Body Paragraph 1

They help form connections in the brain.

They use keywords.

Prompt: Explain how mind maps improve learning.

Body Paragraph 2

Supporting Point 2: Mind maps develop essay writing skills.

They help improve essay structure.

They make your writing clearer.

They organize your thoughts.

Rephrased Thesis Statement: Particular learning elements, including fact recall, essay writing skills, and motivation, are all improved when mind maps are used.

Conclusion

They make complex information easy to understand.

Body Paragraph 3

Supporting Point 3: Mind maps enhance motivation.

They are interactive.

They encourage creativity.

Claim: Mind maps improve learning.

(Cunnah, 2020a; Cunnah, 2020b; Farrand et al., 2002; Goodnough & Woods, 2002; Greene, n.d.; Holland et al., 2003)

Lesson 3.3 Exercise: Mind Map Essay Outline

Instructions: Using the example in Lesson 3.3 as a guide, create a mind map with your own essay outline. Start by writing down your essay prompt in the center, then draw branches and bubbles as needed.

Prompt:

Lesson 3.4: Timeline Graphic Organizer

Are You Ordering a Sequence of Events?

Timelines are the ideal graphic organizer if you're looking to present events in chronological order in your essay. For example, if you're writing a history essay, putting historical events in order could add great structure and organization to your paper.

A timeline graphic organizer is a fantastic outlining method when you're writing a narrative essay because you need to tell a story. It can help your reader understand your narrative essay if it's written in time order. And *don't worry.* You'll learn what a narrative essay is in Chapter 6.

If you're writing an essay about a particular person, you could use this method to map it out, with sections like childhood, adolescence, and adult life.

Here is an example of a timeline graphic organizer used for a history essay. Study this example, so you can use this outlining method to your advantage when appropriate.

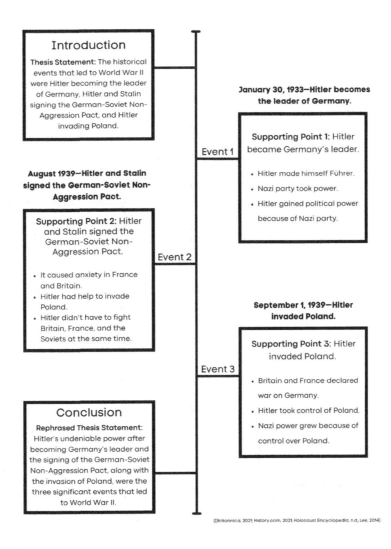

((Britannica, 2021; History.com, 2021; Holocaust Encyclopedia, n.d.; Lee, 2014)

Lesson 3.4 Exercise: Timeline Graphic Organizer

Instructions: Following the example in Lesson 3.4 for guidance, create an outline for your essay by filling out the timeline.

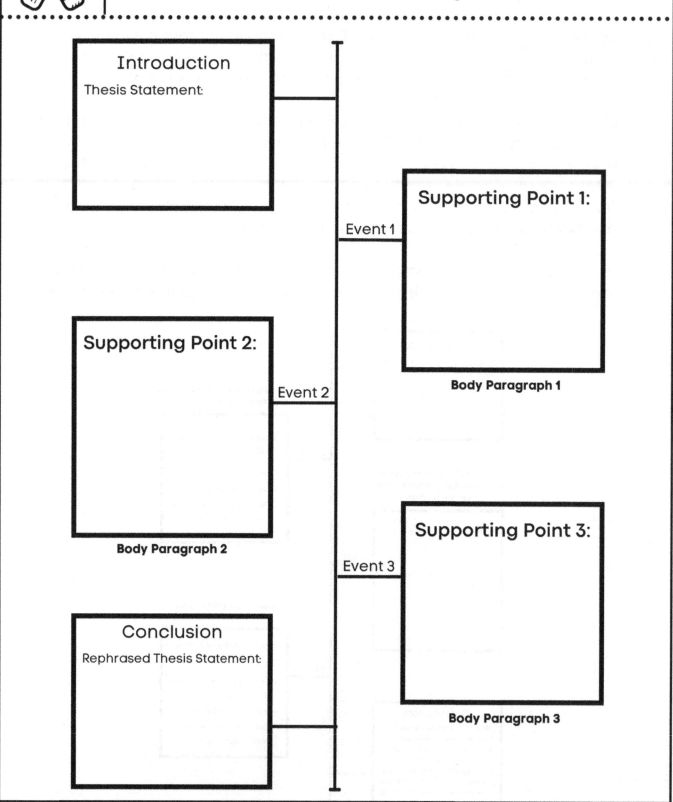

Introduction
Thesis Statement:

Event 1

Supporting Point 1:

Body Paragraph 1

Supporting Point 2:

Event 2

Body Paragraph 2

Event 3

Supporting Point 3:

Body Paragraph 3

Conclusion
Rephrased Thesis Statement:

Lesson 3.5: Flowchart

Find Some Flow!

Like timeline graphic organizers, flowcharts are good for sequences of events. They're also the best choice if you're describing a process or multiple steps.

This is a great option when planning your outline for a persuasive essay, as you can add more and more points to your argument to support your thesis statement.

Let's look at an example!

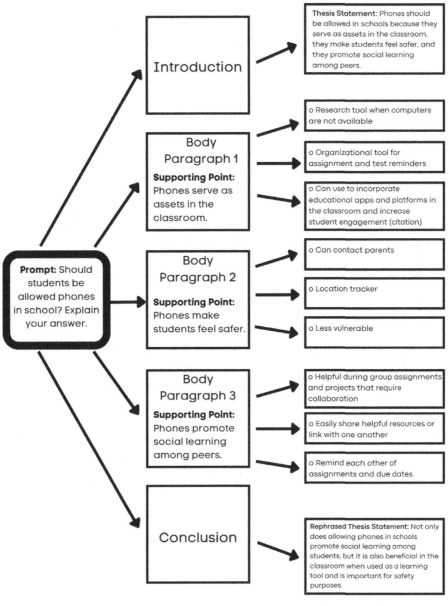

(IvyPanda, 2019; LiveScience, 2008; Tesco Mobile, 2017)

Lesson 3.5 Exercise: Flow Chart Essay Outline

Instructions: Work through the empty flow chart, filling out each section of your essay outline. Take a look at the example in Lesson 3.5 for help!

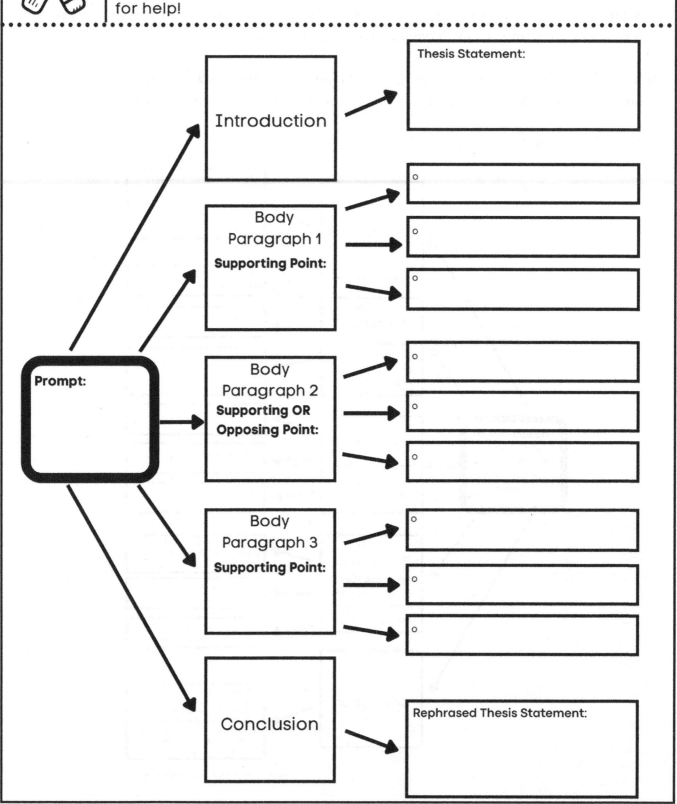

Introduction → Thesis Statement:

Prompt:

Body Paragraph 1 **Supporting Point:** → ○ / ○ / ○

Body Paragraph 2 **Supporting OR Opposing Point:** → ○ / ○ / ○

Body Paragraph 3 **Supporting Point:** → ○ / ○ / ○

Conclusion → Rephrased Thesis Statement:

Chapter 3 Comprehension Quiz

Instructions: Circle the best answer.

1. **What is an outline?**
    a. A way for you to organize your thoughts before you begin writing
    b. A method used to do research on your topic
    c. Tracing the outer part of a drawing
    d. A piece of paper where you brainstorm ideas

2. **What are three benefits of outlining?**
    a. Less time spent writing the essay
    b. Writing will be clearer
    c. Helps to organize your thoughts
    d. All of the above

3. **Why would you use graphic organizers?**
    a. They make learning fun and interactive.
    b. They simplify information.
    c. They improve concentration.
    d. All of the above

4. **What should be included in the introduction section of your outline?**
    a. Supporting/opposing points
    b. Thesis statement
    c. Rephrased thesis statement
    d. Both A and B

5. **What should be included in the body paragraph sections of your outline?**
    a. Thesis statement
    b. Bullet points
    c. Supporting/opposing points
    d. Both B and C

Chapter 3 Comprehension Quiz

Instructions: Circle the best answer.

6. **What should be included in the conclusion section of your outline?**
    a. Rephrased thesis statement
    b. An opinion
    c. A new supporting point
    d. New information

7. **If you have a clashing phrase in your prompt, what should the outline have?**
    a. Introduction, three supporting points, conclusion
    b. Introduction, three opposing points, conclusion
    c. Introduction, two supporting points, one opposing point, conclusion
    d. Introduction, two opposing points, one supporting point, conclusion

8. **What situation is a timeline graphic organizer best for?**
    a. Writing things in a random order
    b. Writing a persuasive essay
    c. Writing for a big audience
    d. Writing events in chronological order

9. **What have mind maps been scientifically proven to do?**
    a. Improve memory of factual information
    b. Make essay writing clearer
    c. Improve essay structure
    d. All of the above

10. **When would you use a flowchart?**
    a. When writing a sequence of events
    b. When writing a process (step-by-step)
    c. When writing events in a random order
    d. Both A and B

STEP 3
Drafting

STEP 3

CHAPTER 4

Getting to the Meat and Potatoes: Writing Your Essay

You have your thesis statement. You've developed your supporting or opposing points. You've created a detailed outline, so now you know what to include in each paragraph.

It's time to write.

This chapter focuses on Step 3: Drafting. In Chapter 1, you read about the different parts of a five-paragraph essay, so the concepts aren't new to you.

In this chapter, we go through them in more depth. We give you easy-to-follow guidance to support you through each and every aspect of drafting an essay.

So, what exactly will we take a look at? We'll explore these topics:

4.1.   How to Write a Compelling Essay Introduction
      4.1.1. Write an Attention-Grabbing Hook

As you can see, this chapter is full to the brim with helpful guidance for you.

Let's get cracking!

Lesson 4.1: How to Write a Compelling Essay Introduction

When it gets down to writing your essay, the first paragraph is the introduction. The introductory paragraph is there to get the reader's attention. You want to draw them in and then reveal what the essay is about. An introduction needs to be clear and concise because the reader won't keep reading if it's long and drones on.

Think: strong words, short sentences, and a clear purpose.

An introduction should *always* include

- a *hook*,
- background information, and
- your thesis statement.

We'll go through each of these in more detail in the following lessons. But first, let's look at an example paragraph, so you can get comfortable identifying the separate elements that make up an introduction.

Prompt: Should students be given homework?

<u>Homework has been around for 116 years!</u> *Homework is assigned schoolwork students are expected to do at home. Teachers give students homework to improve their learning, but it has been a controversial topic for a long time.* **Students should not be given homework because it destroys the home/school balance, increases their stress levels, and reduces time spent with family and friends** (Teachnology, Inc, n.d.)**.**

So, which part do you think was the hook? The hook was the short, snappy first sentence that's underlined. It grabs your attention by giving you a shocking statistic. Then comes the background information in italics. The sentence in bold is the thesis statement, which is easy to identify when you look for the three supporting points.

Lesson 4.1.1: Write an Attention-Grabbing Hook

The hook is the very first sentence of your essay. Its role is simple: Get the reader's attention (Matthews, 2020, p. 40). This is when the reader decides whether they want to read the rest of your essay or not. So, your first sentence needs to be interesting. It also needs to be short and punchy because long, drawn-out first sentences are boring!

Remember to highlight the main focus of your essay in your hook because you want to lead the reader nicely into the rest of your essay.

There isn't just one type of hook; there are lots! You can choose whichever one you think works best with your prompt.

Your hook can be a

- fascinating question,
- short explanation of the essay topic's importance,
- clever quote,
- shocking fact or statistic, or
- contradiction.

 Study Skill: Remember, if you're writing an exact quote, fact, or statistic, don't forget the reference!

Let's check out some examples of hooks. The first hook needs some work. Can you see the improvement in the second version?

1. There are lots of McDonald's all over the world.
2. McDonald's has taken over every continent apart from Antarctica.

This is a shocking *fact* hook. The first version is vague and not very interesting. The second version, however, is surprising, making you want to read more.

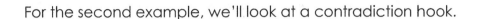

For the second example, we'll look at a contradiction hook.

1. Animals are important, but people don't treat them that way.
2. Animals are vital to human existence, yet we continue to mistreat them.

The first version uses generalized language that doesn't stand out to the reader. The second, improved version uses punchy words like "vital" and "mistreat," which trigger strong emotions in the reader.

In the table, you'll find examples of the other three types of hooks:

Type of Hook	Example
Fascinating Question	Are you getting too much sun?
Short Explanation of the Topic's Importance	To keep your muscles strong and flexible, you must stretch regularly.
Clever Quote	"Innovation distinguishes between a leader and a follower." —Steve Jobs

Now, a hook doesn't have to be a question *or* a fact *or* a contradiction (and so on). Sometimes, a hook can be a combination of two things. Here's an example:

Vitamin D is essential if you want to keep your body in tip-top condition!

This is an explanation of the essay topic's importance *and* an interesting fact.

 Study Skill: If you're using a quote, try not to quote the dictionary. These definitions tend to be long and unexciting!

Lesson 4.1.1 Exercise: Improve the Hooks

Instructions: This exercise includes hooks that still need some work. Identify what type of hook they are and improve each hook so it grabs the reader's attention.

Example

Hook 1: Are people eating too much sugar?

Type of Hook: A question

New and Improved: Do you eat too much sugar?

Hook 2: Family is important.

Type of Hook: _____

New and Improved: _____

_____

Hook 3: Heart disease kills lots of women in the United States.

Type of Hook: _____

New and Improved: _____

_____

Hook 4: What are the different factors necessary to make a student successful?

Type of Hook: _____

New and Improved: _____

_____

Hook 5: A lot of people plan to get fit, but they can't convince themselves to get off the couch and put some work in.

Type of Hook: _____

New and Improved: _____

_____

Lesson 4.1.1 Exercise: Improve the Hooks

Instructions: This exercise includes hooks that still need some work. Identify what type of hook they are, and improve each hook so it grabs the reader's attention.

Hook 6: Carolyn Birmingham said, "A smile starts on the lips, a grin spreads to the eyes, a chuckle comes from the belly; but a good laugh bursts forth from the soul, overflows, and bubbles all around."

Type of Hook: _____

New and Improved: _____

_____

Hook 7: Did you know dogs are the number one household pet in the U.S.?

Type of Hook: _____

New and Improved: _____

_____

Hook 8: Outer space is big, making it important.

Type of Hook: _____

New and Improved: _____

_____

Hook 9: Humans want to stay safe but then drive over the speed limit.

Type of Hook: _____

New and Improved: _____

_____

What type of hook do you want to use? _____

Your Hook: _____

_____

Lesson 4.1.2: Give Background Information

After the hook comes the background information. Background information adds context to your introductory paragraph, giving general information about the essay topic that helps build the reader's knowledge.

In other words, it's the detail you provide so your reader can fully understand the focus of your essay.

Background information comes in many forms:

- Definitions
- Facts
- Current events
- Opinions (positive, negative, or opposite)
- Statistics
- Relevant history

Imagine you were writing about preparing for an earthquake. Let's go over each type of background information using this example.

Essay Prompt: Explain in detail how someone can prepare for an earthquake.

- **Definition:** An earthquake is an aggressive trembling of the ground caused by movement of the Earth's crust (Bolt, 2021).
- **Fact:** An earthquake can change the length of a day (BBC, 2017).
- **Current Events:** In 2020, there were 938 earthquakes in Oklahoma, Texas, Louisiana, and New Mexico alone (Insurance Journal, 2021).

- **Opinions:** Many people are ill-prepared for these life-threatening situations.
- **Statistics:** Ten thousand U.S. citizens die from earthquakes annually (National Geographic, 2021).
- **Relevant History:** The first earthquake was described in China in 1177 B.C. (U.S. Department of the Interior, 2016).

You want to pick two to four of these pieces of information to use in your introduction. They must all be related to your thesis statement. The last portion of background information should lead smoothly into your thesis statement.

You can pull from the research you've already done to scrounge up information and piece it together for this section of the introduction. Feel free to conduct more research if necessary.

Here's what it looks like when we put some pieces of background information together:

{Background Information} An earthquake is an aggressive trembling of the ground caused by movement of the Earth's crust, and descriptive records show they occurred as early as 1177 B.C. in China (Bolt, 2021; U.S. Department of the Interior, 2016). Fast-forwarding to modern times, in 2020 there were 938 earthquakes in Oklahoma, Texas, Louisiana, and New Mexico alone (Insurance Journal, 2021). Despite these common occurrences, many people are still ill-prepared for these life-threatening situations.

 Study Skill: You may have to rearrange the wording of some of your facts to get a good flow.

Let's come up with an attention-grabbing hook for this example and put them together. If you look carefully, we could use the statistic we found for the background information as an interesting statistic hook instead because it has that *shock* factor and was not used as part of the background information:

{Hook} An average of ten thousand people around the globe die from earthquakes every year (National Geographic, 2021). **{Background Information}** An earthquake is an aggressive trembling of the ground caused by movement of the Earth's crust, and descriptive records show they occurred as early as 1177 B.C. in China (Bolt, 2021; U.S. Department of the Interior, 2016). Fast-forwarding to modern times, in 2020 there were 938 earthquakes in Oklahoma, Texas, Louisiana, and New Mexico alone (Insurance Journal, 2021). Despite these common occurrences, many people are still ill-prepared for these life-threatening situations.

Background Information No-Nos

You now know what background information *should* look like, but what about what it *shouldn't* include?

Background information should not include the following:

- Personal opinions with no evidence behind them (unless you're writing an informal essay that's based on opinion and nonfactual information).
- Information that doesn't relate to the prompt.

Let's take a look at some examples:

1. I think earthquakes are dangerous.

   You can transform this uninformative opinion into usable background information with the help of reliable sources:

   Earthquakes are extremely dangerous, as they can topple buildings and cause tsunamis (BBC, 2011).

2. Tornadoes cause a lot of destruction.

   At the moment, this statement has nothing to do with earthquakes. You can, however, adapt this to make it relevant:

   Earthquakes are considered a natural disaster, much like tornadoes and tsunamis.

Lesson 4.1.2 Exercise: Match Up

Instructions: Draw a line from each sentence to the type of background information it is.

Background Information

1. The number of online shoppers in the United States has risen from 209.6 million in 2016 to 230.5 million in 2021 (Coppola, 2021).

2. Some people believe purple is the best color while others argue it's blue.

3. Pizza first became a hit in ancient cultures, where it started off as a flatbread with different toppings.

4. Recently, numerous wildfires have disrupted the state of California.

5. Peace is defined as "a state or period in which there is no war or a war has ended" (Lexico, n.d.).

6. For a short period, New York was called "New Orange" (Ephemeral New York, 2011).

Type

Current events

Statistic

Definition

Fact

Relevant history

Opinion

Lesson 4.1.2 Exercise: Background Bonanza

Instructions: Find some background information for your essay prompt! The first table is based off Lesson 4.1.2.

Essay Prompt: Explain in detail how someone can prepare for an earthquake.

Type of Background Information	Background Information Sentence
Definition	An earthquake is aggressive trembling of the ground caused by movement of the Earth's crust (Bolt, 2021).
Fact	An earthquake can change the length of a day (BBC, 2017).
Current Event	In 2020, there were 938 earthquakes in Oklahoma, Texas, Louisiana, and New Mexico alone (Insurance Journal, 2021).
Opinion	Many people are ill-prepared for these life-threatening situations.
Statistic	Ten thousand U.S. citizens die from earthquakes annually (National Geographic, 2021).
Relevant History	Descriptive records show earthquakes occurred as early as 1177 B.C. in China (U.S. Department of the Interior, 2016).

Lesson 4.1.2 Exercise: Background Bonanza

Instructions: Find some background information for your essay prompt! The first table is based off Lesson 4.1.2.

Essay Prompt: _____

Type of Background Information	Background Information Sentence
Definition	
Fact	
Current Event	
Opinion	
Statistic	
Relevant History	

Lesson 4.1.3: Thesis Statement Review

We explored thesis statements in a lot of detail in Lesson 2.8. Don't worry—we won't go over it all again!

Let's recap what we covered. If you need to remind yourself of thesis statements in more depth or get a little more practice, you can go back to Lesson 2.8 and Lesson 2.8 Exercise!

What Is a Thesis Statement Again?

A thesis statement is a sentence that brings together the central ideas of your essay. It goes after your background information to finish off your introductory paragraph.

Your thesis statement should be a combination of your claim and your three supporting points (or opposing points). Have you got yours ready?

Going back to the earthquake prompt, here is a possible thesis statement:

The three most important ways an individual can prepare for an earthquake are making a plan, identifying safe spaces indoors and outdoors, and having emergency supplies.

Let's finish the introductory paragraph by adding the hook, background information, and thesis statement together:

{Hook} An average of ten thousand people around the globe die from earthquakes every year (National Geographic, 2021). **{Background Information}** An earthquake is an aggressive trembling of the ground caused by movement of the Earth's crust, and descriptive records show they occurred as early as 1177 B.C. in China (Bolt, 2021; U.S. Department of the Interior, 2016). Fast-forwarding to modern times, in 2020 there were 938 earthquakes in Oklahoma, Texas, Louisiana, and New Mexico alone (Insurance Journal, 2021). Despite these common occurrences, many people are still ill-prepared for these life-threatening situations. **{Thesis Statement}** The three most important ways an individual can prepare for an earthquake are making a plan, identifying safe spaces indoors and outdoors, and having emergency supplies.

Study Skill: The last portion of background information should lead smoothly into your thesis statement. Do you see how the second to last sentence effortlessly leads into the thesis statement in the introduction example?

End-of-Lesson 4.1 Exercise: Identify The Parts

Instructions: Underline the hook, circle the background information, and draw a squiggly line under the thesis statement for each introduction paragraph. Write your own introduction for the last question.

① **Prompt: Why do people stereotype strangers? Explain your reasoning.**

Do you stereotype? Whether you like it or not, you stereotype people every single day. Stereotyping is when you assume something about a stranger's personality, appearance, or life in general. Science has repeatedly proven that stereotyping is not accurate. People stereotype because it brings order to the brain, it is a survival instinct, and it allows them to respond quickly to surprising situations.

② **Prompt: Describe whether you agree or disagree with the following statement: You need money to be happy.**

"Money can't buy happiness, but it can make you awfully comfortable while you're being miserable." This short and sweet quote from author and politician Clare Boothe Luce says it all. Everyone wants to be happy, and happiness is often linked with money. This urges people to chase after money, like a cat after a mouse. However, money can't buy happiness because the positive feeling from money is only short-term, material things don't bring happiness, and you can't buy friendship.

③ **Prompt: The legal age to drive in many U.S. states is 16. Discuss the positives and negatives of this law.**

From 2010 to 2019 there were 18,252 driving fatalities of teens between 15 and 20 years old in the U.S. (Insurance Information Institute, n.d.). It has long been debated whether 16 is too young to be driving. Even though 16-year-olds are still developing mentally, they should be allowed to drive because a driver's license increases their transportation options and fosters new experiences that will help them build life skills.

End-of-Lesson 4.1 Exercise: Identify The Parts

Instructions: Underline the hook, circle the background information, and draw a squiggly line under the thesis statement for each introduction paragraph. Write your own introduction for the last question.

④ **Prompt: Some people believe there's no point in reading fiction. Do you agree or disagree with this opinion?**

Did you know reading increases vocabulary and boosts communication skills? Despite these benefits, many people believe reading fiction is a waste of time. Fiction is literature that colorfully describes imaginary events, characters, worlds, and magical scenarios. Even though fiction does not directly relate to real life, people should read fiction because it teaches you to infer and interpret, it strengthens comprehension skills, and it enhances creativity.

⑤ **Your Prompt:** _____

_____

Your Introduction: _____

_____

_____

_____

_____

_____

_____

Lesson 4.2: Adding the Patty to the Buns: How to Build Body Paragraphs for Your Essay

You've reeled the audience in with an intriguing introduction, and now it's time for the body paragraphs. The body paragraphs are where you use evidence (aka *supporting information*) to argue your thesis statement. Body paragraphs need to do these three things:

- Relate to your claim

  Keep it clear and to the point! It's easy to go off on a tangent when writing your body paragraphs. To avoid this, ask, "Could I remove this paragraph without affecting my argument?" If the answer is yes, you need to take another look at it. It needs to be an essential part of your essay. Otherwise, it's not adding value!

- Present one idea only

  Bringing in multiple ideas will confuse the reader. Stick to one idea per paragraph!

- Be a good length—not too long, not too short!

  You want a body paragraph with enough evidence to support the claim, but not so much that your reader stops paying attention! One-sentence paragraphs may look cool and require less work, but that won't help you become a better writer.

All body paragraphs are made up of four essential elements:

1. Topic sentence
2. Evidence (aka *supporting information*)
3. Analysis
4. Concluding sentence

We stick to this structure, keeping it the same for all the body paragraphs, because this makes your essay more organized and gives it a nice flow. It also makes it predictable, so the reader knows what to expect.

This lesson goes over writing body paragraphs when using three supporting points. Don't fret if you have a clashing phrase in your prompt, however! Later, we will address how to write counterargument body paragraphs, which are important when you have two supporting points and one opposing point. Nonetheless, it's imperative to understand the fundamentals before we get there. So, don't skip through these lessons. The material builds on itself!

Whether you're writing a supporting or counterargument body paragraph, there are four easy steps for creating a body paragraph:

1. Form a topic sentence.
2. Bring in the evidence.
3. Analyze your evidence.
4. Add a concluding sentence.

We will go through these in detail in the next few lessons.

Lesson 4.2.1: Tackling the Topic Sentence

A topic sentence is typically the very first sentence of your body paragraph. It performs a couple of jobs:

1. It tells the reader the main idea of the paragraph.
2. It improves the flow of the essay.

If a topic sentence hits these targets, it's bound to be a good one. But don't be fooled into thinking a topic sentence must be a single sentence. It can be multiple! However, we recommend sticking to two or less, or your paragraph will end up being too long!

Forming Your Topic Sentence

You will go through two simple steps to create your topic sentence.

Step 1: Revisiting Your Outline

When tackling the topic sentence, your first task is to look back over your outline. Remember in Lesson 2.7 we explored supporting points? Well, these are going to come in handy here.

The three supporting points you came up with will form the main ideas of your three body paragraphs, one supporting point per body paragraph. This should be clear from your outline. You'll use these supporting points to help craft your topic sentences. As such, your topic sentence should relate back to one of the three points in your *thesis statement*.

Do you remember our earthquake example from Lesson 4.1.3? Let's pick out the supporting points from the thesis.

Prompt: Explain in detail how someone can prepare for an earthquake.

Thesis Statement: The three most important ways an individual can prepare for an earthquake are <u>making a plan</u>, <u>identifying safe spaces indoors and outdoors</u>, and <u>having emergency supplies</u>.

Here, the supporting points are underlined.

- Body Paragraph 1 → Supporting Point 1: Making a plan
- Body Paragraph 2 → Supporting Point 2: Identifying safe spaces indoors and outdoors
- Body Paragraph 3 → Supporting Point 3: Having emergency supplies

Step 2: Supporting Point to Topic Sentence

When creating your topic sentence, make sure to do the following:

- Relate back to your supporting point
- Be clear and concise (no long, drawn out sentences!)
- Be specific to your prompt, without telling the reader everything

Try to avoid these pitfalls:

- Presenting the reader with common knowledge
- Using a basic, uninteresting fact
- Using quotes

Using the example of earthquakes, let's compare a great topic sentence to one that needs more work.

Needs Work: Making a plan is an important step.

Although this topic sentence mentions the point of the paragraph, it doesn't relate back to the prompt. Also, the sentence isn't very interesting or specific.

Improved: Earthquakes can strike unexpectedly, so making a plan is an important step that an individual can take to prepare for one.

This topic sentence ticks all the boxes because it mentions the main idea of the paragraph and references the focus of the overall essay. It is also specific to your essay without telling the reader everything.

Let's try this for the second supporting point: identifying safe spaces indoors and out.

Needs Work: This paragraph presents another way to stay safe from earthquakes.

This topic sentence relates back to the prompt by mentioning earthquakes, but it doesn't present the main idea of the paragraph! Also, saying phrases like "this paragraph presents" seems clumsy. Your paragraph should be so good the reader knows what's being presented!

Improved: It's imperative to prepare for earthquakes by identifying safe spaces indoors and outdoors, as this trick can be the difference between life and death.

This improved version mentions the paragraph's main idea and refers back to the prompt. It doesn't need to spell out what it presents because the language is clear.

Tips on Topic Sentences

1. **Don't tell the reader what you're doing.**

   Example

   Now I will talk about why making a plan is important.

   You want to guide your reader through your ideas without explicitly telling them what you're doing.

2. **Don't be too specific OR too general.**

   If your topic sentence is too specific, you won't have enough to write about in your paragraph. If it's too general, you'll have way too much to write about!

   Find the sweet spot in the middle.

Examples

Too Specific: Collecting emergency supplies, such as a list of emergency contact numbers, a flashlight, drinks, and snacks can help an individual prepare for an earthquake.

Yes, this sentence is very informative. But it doesn't leave a lot for you to talk about in the rest of the paragraph, does it?

Too General: Use supplies during earthquakes.

Reading this, your reader won't know what you're talking about! The main idea here isn't clear because the topic sentence isn't specific. Additionally, you could write an endless amount of information for this paragraph. Instead, try a sentence like this:

Improved: Having an emergency supply kit readied ahead of time is yet another way to prepare for an earthquake.

Here, the main idea is presented clearly, and the prompt is referenced.

3. **Present a reasonable idea.**

No reader is going to continue reading your essay if your ideas are too extreme. Also, extreme, outlandish ideas are difficult to prove. You need to present a reasonable idea, so you can give evidence that proves it in your body paragraph.

Don't write a topic sentence that is only facts. The facts will come into play when we add the supporting information to the paragraph.

Lesson 4.2.1 Exercise: Test Your Topic Sentence Skills

Instructions: You're given three prompts with their corresponding thesis statements. Write a topic sentence for each main idea in the thesis statement.

① **Prompt**: Is play important in childhood? Explain your reasoning.

Thesis Statement: Play is important in childhood because it aids the development of fine motor skills, teaches children how to problem solve, and builds social interaction skills.

Topic Sentence 1: _____
_____
_____

Topic Sentence 2: _____
_____
_____

Topic Sentence 3: _____
_____
_____

② **Prompt**: Why should teenagers have their own rooms?

Thesis Statement: Teenagers should have their own rooms because it gives them quiet time, privacy, and independence.

Topic Sentence 1: _____
_____
_____

Topic Sentence 2: _____
_____
_____

Topic Sentence 3: _____
_____
_____

Lesson 4.2.1 Exercise: Test Your Topic Sentence Skills

Instructions: You're given three prompts with their corresponding thesis statements. Write a topic sentence for each main idea in the thesis statement.

③ **Prompt**: What is the best movie snack? Explain.

Thesis Statement: Popcorn is by far the best movie snack because it is buttery, salty, and satisfyingly crunchy.

Topic Sentence 1: _____

_____

_____

Topic Sentence 2: _____

_____

_____

Topic Sentence 3: _____

_____

_____

④ **Your Prompt:** _____

Your Thesis Statement: _____

_____

Topic Sentence 1: _____

_____

_____

Topic Sentence 2: _____

_____

_____

Topic Sentence 3: _____

_____

Lesson 4.2.2: Establishing Evidence

The next step of writing a body paragraph is establishing evidence, which we can also refer to as *supporting information*. This step involves elaborating on the topic sentence and giving evidence to support it. Your evidence needs to relate to your thesis statement *as well as* your specific topic sentence; otherwise, it won't make much sense.

Study Skill: Remember, when you're providing evidence from outside sources, you need references!

Supporting information can include the following:

- Examples
- Scientific studies/research
- Statistics
- Facts
- Anecdotes
- Quotations (especially if you're writing a book report or a literary essay)

*This is not an exhaustive list.

Don't worry; you're not starting from scratch! If you followed along in Chapter 3, you should have some bullet points in the body paragraph sections of your outline. These bullet points were based on questions like these:

- How does your supporting point relate to your claim?
- How does your supporting point reinforce and support your claim?
- Why is your supporting point important or true?

*Look at lesson 3.1 for a visual refresher of these bullet points in the example outline.

Do you remember? We're going to adapt those bullet points here to form your evidence.

If you were to use the earthquake prompt example, you might have bullet points like this in the Body Paragraph 1 section of your outline:

Thesis Statement: The three most important ways an individual can prepare for an earthquake are making a plan, identifying safe spaces indoors and outdoors, and having emergency supplies.

Topic Sentence: Earthquakes can strike unexpectedly, so making a plan is an important step that an individual can take to prepare for one.

Body Paragraph 1 ➔ Supporting Point 1: Making a plan

Know what to do
- Reduce stress
- Wider community benefit

*Think about how making a plan prepares you for an earthquake. How does this supporting point *reinforce* the claim?

To transform these bullet points into essay-worthy information that supports your topic sentence and acts as evidence, you need to make them into full, coherent sentences, like this:

Evidence 1 ➔ Being properly equipped with a well-thought-out strategy and knowing what to do prevents scrambling around out of fear.

Evidence 2 ➔ Planning ahead for disasters can reduce stress and alleviate anxiety.

Evidence 3 ➔ Making a plan can help minimize damage on a wider community scale (Federal Emergency Management Agency [FEMA], 2009).

Here, three statements supporting the topic sentence are clearly presented.

If your bulleted points were already full sentences from your outline or graphic organizer, they will serve as your evidence. However, make sure your sentences are essay-ready by strengthening them or changing wording around as needed.

Again, these sentences will serve as evidence that directly follows your topic sentence. You don't need to transform all the bullet points you come up with in your outline to use as evidence in your essay.

Use as much or as little needed to prove the claim you made in the topic sentence. You might end up using all three bullet points, two bullet points, or maybe just one! Use your best judgment. For the purposes of our example, we chose to transform all three bullet points into full sentences to show you the process.

Now that we've looked at an *ideal* example of some supporting information and evidence, let's look at one that needs some work:

Thesis Statement: The three most important ways an individual can prepare for an earthquake are making a plan, identifying safe spaces indoors and outdoors, and having emergency supplies.

Topic Sentence: Earthquakes can strike unexpectedly, so making a plan is an important step that an individual can take to prepare for one.

> **Body Paragraph 1 ➜ Supporting Point 1:** Making a plan
>
> Fun and helpful
>
> *Think about how making a plan prepares you for an earthquake. How does this supporting point *reinforce* the claim?

Evidence ➜ Making plans ahead of time is fun and helpful for most people.

What's wrong with this evidence?

It doesn't relate to the topic sentence for this body paragraph because it doesn't pertain to earthquakes or being prepared at all. It only mentions *making plans* in the context of being fun and helpful, which isn't specific to the topic sentence, thesis statement, or essay! It's also clear that the one sentence here wouldn't be enough to support the claim in the topic sentence. This is not a sufficient amount of evidence in this case.

So, when you're writing your evidence, make sure you relate it back to your claim, use an appropriate amount of evidence, and include references when appropriate! We'll talk about references later in this chapter.

Before we move onto the next lesson, let's tack on the evidence to our topic sentence to start forming our body paragraph! Note we only used one piece of evidence instead of all three because it's sufficient to support the claim in the topic sentence:

{**Topic Sentence**} Earthquakes can strike unexpectedly, so making a plan is an important step that an individual can take to prepare for one. {**Evidence**} Being properly equipped with a well-thought-out strategy and knowing what to do prevents scrambling around out of fear (FEMA, 2009).

Lesson 4.2.2 Exercise: Transform the Bullet Points

Instructions: You've been given one bullet point per question. Your task is to transform the bullet points into essay-ready evidence!

① **Prompt:** Explain the physical health benefits of walking.

Claim: Walking is beneficial for physical health.
Body Paragraph → Supporting Point: Reduces risk of heart disease
• Stronger heart

*Think about how reducing risk of heart disease is beneficial for physical health. How does this supporting point reinforce the claim?

{Topic Sentence} Walking is good for your physical health because it reduces the risk of heart disease.

Evidence: _____

_____

_____

_____

_____

_____

② **Prompt:** Describe how current road safety campaigns improve safety.

Claim: Current road safety campaigns improve safety.
Body Paragraph → Supporting Point: Make drivers more aware of risks
• Less likely to take risks

*Think about how drivers being more aware of driving risks improves road safety. How does this supporting point reinforce the claim?

{Topic Sentence} Current road safety campaigns improve safety because they make drivers more aware of driving risks.

Evidence: _____

_____

_____

_____

_____

Lesson 4.2.2 Exercise: Transform the Bullet Points

Instructions: You've been given one bullet point per question. Your task is to transform the bullet points into essay-ready evidence!

③ **Prompt:** Some parents stop children from trick-or-treating at Halloween. Do you agree or disagree with this decision?

Claim: Children should be allowed to trick-or-treat.
Body Paragraph → Supporting Point: Gets kids outside
• Physically active

*Think about how getting kids outside is an argument for allowing children to trick-or-treat. How does this supporting point reinforce the claim?

{Topic Sentence} Children should be allowed to trick-or-treat because it gets them outside.

Evidence: _____
_____
_____
_____
_____
_____

④ **Prompt:** What is the best writing instrument? Explain your reasoning.

Claim: Mechanical pencils are the best writing instrument.
Body Paragraph → Supporting Point: Last longer than traditional pencils
• Do not need to be sharpened

*Think about how mechanical pencils lasting longer than traditional pencils make them the best writing instrument. How does this supporting point reinforce the claim?

{Topic Sentence} Mechanical pencils are the best writing instruments because they last longer than traditional wooden pencils.

Evidence: _____
_____
_____
_____
_____
_____

Lesson 4.2.2 Exercise: Transform the Bullet Points

Instructions: Now, it's your turn to transform your own bullet points into evidence for your body paragraphs!

Your Prompt:

Your Claim:

Body Paragraph 1 → Supporting Point 1:
*

Evidence: _____
_____
_____
_____
_____
_____

Body Paragraph 2 → Supporting Point 1:
*

Evidence: _____
_____
_____
_____
_____

Body Paragraph 3 → Supporting Point 3 OR Opposing Point:
*

Evidence: _____
_____
_____
_____
_____

Lesson 4.2.3: Analysis

You've given the reader the supporting information, but in order for your reader to really see the connection between the evidence and the topic sentence, you need to *analyze* the information.

You do this by asking, "How does the evidence I provided *prove* the topic sentence?" Remember, your topic sentence really just expresses one of your supporting points.

You need to analyze the evidence you present in a body paragraph.

Check out the different ways to present analysis and the examples related to our earthquake prompt. You can use one or multiple methods of analysis in your body paragraph. Your analysis may end up being multiple sentences.

Here, we'll take Evidence 1 from the previous lesson to analyze using the different methods:

Being properly equipped with a well-thought-out strategy and knowing what to do prevents scrambling around out of fear.

Method 1: *Explain → Make it clear what your supporting information means and how it relates to the topic sentence.*

Example: The ultimate aim when facing a natural disaster is security. Making a plan keeps you safe, so it's essential when preparing for an earthquake.

Method 2: *Expand → Add detail to your supporting information.*

Example: This will make your response more efficient and allow you to take cover quickly.

Method 3: *Interpret → Describe what your supporting information means in reference to your thesis statement.*

Example: If a carefully constructed plan helps you stay safe, the earthquake will have less of an impact.

Isn't Evidence Self-Explanatory?

Sometimes, evidence can seem like it doesn't need to be explained further with an analysis. There are two reasons why you should analyze your evidence:

1. It may not be as obvious to the reader.

    You know what your evidence means because you're the one who found it. But, imagine you're a reader who knows nothing about the topic. You'd need an explanation as to why the evidence relates to the overall thesis statement, right?

2. It shows the reader you really know what you're talking about.

    Analysis gives you a chance to show how your evidence relates to the main idea of your paragraph. It also provides an opportunity for you to show how it links back to your overall thesis statement. By linking everything together, the reader can see you have a real understanding of the topic.

Let's combine our analysis with what we have so far for our body paragraph:

{Topic Sentence} Earthquakes can strike unexpectedly, so making a plan is an important step that an individual can take to prepare for one. **{Evidence}** Being properly equipped with a well-thought-out strategy and knowing what to do prevents scrambling around out of fear (FEMA, 2009). **{Analysis}** This will make your response more efficient and allow you to take cover quickly. If a carefully constructed plan helps you stay safe, the earthquake will have less of an impact.

Sometimes, when you put your sentences together, they can seem a bit clumsy. You may need to try rewriting your sentences and removing words to get a good sense of flow in your paragraph.

*Study Skill: Don't think you can get away with just saying "this supports the claim" in your analysis—this doesn't tell the reader **how** it supports the claim.*

Lesson 4.2.3 Exercise: Add the Analysis

Instructions: You've been given a partial paragraph with a topic sentence and evidence. Your job is to add the analysis.

1 **Prompt:** Explain the physical health benefits of walking.

Claim: Walking is beneficial for physical health.
Body Paragraph → Supporting Point: Reduces risk of heart disease
• Stronger heart

*Think about how reducing risk of heart disease is beneficial for physical health. How does this supporting point reinforce the claim?

{Topic Sentence} Walking is good for your physical health because it reduces the risk of heart disease. {Evidence} The heart is a muscle, and any muscle benefits from exercise, such as walking. A stronger heart can pump more blood around the body with less effort (NHS, 2020).

Analysis: _____
_____
_____
_____

2 **Prompt:** Describe how current road safety campaigns improve safety.

Claim: Current road safety campaigns improve safety.
Body Paragraph → Supporting Point: Make drivers more aware of risks
• Less likely to take risks

*Think about how drivers being more aware of driving risks improves road safety. How does this supporting point reinforce the claim?

{Topic Sentence} Current road safety campaigns improve safety because they make drivers more aware of driving risks. {Evidence} Road safety campaigns teach drivers to wear a seatbelt while driving, to follow the speed limit, and to abide by the rules of the road. Otherwise, motor vehicle accidents and other road mishaps are more likely to occur.

Analysis: _____
_____
_____
_____

Lesson 4.2.3 Exercise: Add the Analysis

Instructions: You've been given a partial paragraph with a topic sentence and evidence. Your job is to add the analysis.

③ **Prompt:** Some parents stop children from trick-or-treating at Halloween. Do you agree or disagree with this decision?

Claim: Children should be allowed to trick-or-treat.
Body Paragraph → Supporting Point: Gets kids outside
• Physically active

*Think about how getting kids outside is an argument for allowing children to trick-or-treat. How does this supporting point reinforce the claim?

{Topic Sentence} Children should be allowed to trick-or-treat because it gets them outside. **{Evidence}** When children are allowed to trick-or-treat, they have a chance to get dressed up, go outside, and be physically active from all the walking between houses. They are able to run around and breathe fresh air, instead of being glued to their phones at home.

Analysis: _____

_____

_____

_____

④ **Prompt:** What is the best writing instrument? Explain your reasoning.

Claim: Mechanical pencils are the best writing instrument.
Body Paragraph → Supporting Point: Last longer than traditional pencils
• Do not need to be sharpened

*Think about how mechanical pencils lasting longer than traditional pencils make them the best writing instrument. How does this supporting point reinforce the claim?

{Topic Sentence} Mechanical pencils are the best writing instruments because they last longer than traditional wooden pencils. **{Evidence}** The lead in mechanical pencils stays a consistent size and does not become dull, while the lead in wooden pencils dulls over time and needs to be regularly sharpened.

Analysis: _____

_____

_____

_____

Lesson 4.2.3 Exercise: Add the Analysis

Instructions: Add the analysis for your own body paragraphs!

Your Prompt:

Your Claim:

Body Paragraph 1 → Supporting Point 1:

Analysis: _____

_____

_____

_____

_____

_____

_____

Body Paragraph 2 → Supporting Point 1:

Analysis: _____

_____

_____

_____

_____

_____

Body Paragraph 3 → Supporting Point 3 OR Opposing Point:

Analysis: _____

_____

_____

_____

_____

_____

Lesson 4.2.4: Concluding Sentence

To wrap up your body paragraph, you want a clear, concise sentence or two telling the reader exactly what the paragraph has proven.

There are two goals you should be striving for when writing your concluding sentence. Don't get this mixed up with your *conclusion*, which will be the last paragraph in your essay.

Now, what are the two goals?

Goal 1: Summarize the Main Idea of Your Paragraph

One purpose of your concluding sentence is to summarize the main idea of your body paragraph.

You just wrote an amazing paragraph, with a spectacular topic sentence, great evidence, and impressive analysis. However, it may be hard for readers to fully understand the meaning of what you are saying. By summarizing the main idea of your paragraph, you stress its importance as a part of your essay's argument. You also refocus the reader's attention to the broader picture, making sure they are not getting hung up on any minor details.

Goal 2: Link Back to Your Thesis Statement

The second goal to keep in mind while writing your concluding sentence is to create a connection to your thesis statement (Matthews, 2020, p. 56).

Students often wonder *why* they have to connect each body paragraph to their thesis statement. After all, it should be obvious, right?

Wrong!

There are three key reasons why you link back to your thesis statement:

1. It shows you haven't just plucked an idea out of nowhere; it does actually relate to the claim of your essay.
2. It demonstrates you haven't forgotten your main idea!
3. It reminds the reader of your claim.

Here's an example of a concluding sentence for our earthquake body paragraph that meets these goals:

It is clear that developing a strategic plan eliminates many hazards during an earthquake and stops panic, and this makes it an effective method of preparation.

Now let's see what our body paragraph looks like altogether. We will include the thesis statement so you can see how the concluding sentence of the body paragraph connects back to the thesis:

Thesis Statement: The three most important ways an individual can prepare for an earthquake are making a plan, identifying safe spaces indoors and outdoors, and having emergency supplies.

Body Paragraph: {Topic Sentence} Earthquakes can strike unexpectedly, so making a plan is an important step that an individual can take to prepare for one. **{Evidence}** Being properly equipped with a well-thought-out strategy and knowing what to do prevents scrambling around out of fear (FEMA, 2009). **{Analysis}** This will make your response more efficient and allow you to take cover quickly. If a carefully constructed plan helps you stay safe, the earthquake will have less of an impact. **{Concluding Sentence}** It is clear that developing a strategic plan eliminates many hazards during an earthquake and stops panic, and this makes it an effective method of preparation.

Do you see how the example concluding sentence summarizes the main idea of the paragraph *and* links back to the thesis statement? Do you see how the claim is still relevant? That's what you want in a concluding sentence.

Lesson 4.2.4 Exercise: Pick the Concluding Sentence

Instructions: For each question, pick the concluding sentence that makes the most sense for the given prompt, claim, thesis statement, and topic sentence.

① **Prompt:** Some people believe aliens exist. Argue for or against this belief.

Claim: Aliens do exist.

Thesis Statement: Aliens must exist within our universe because there are other planets capable of supporting life. Beyond that, there have been many sightings of unidentified objects and several instances of unusual activity in space.

Topic Sentence: Aliens do exist because scientific research has detected unusual activity from space.

A. The government has been hiding evidence of alien life for years.
B. Aliens exist because there have been sightings of them.
C. Years of scientific research detecting unusual activity from space points toward the existence of aliens.

② **Prompt:** Explain the benefits of a vegetarian diet.

Claim: A vegetarian diet is beneficial.

Thesis Statement: A vegetarian diet is a great choice overall, as it lowers blood pressure, lowers grocery costs, and decreases negative environmental impact.

Topic Sentence: People don't usually think of the financial benefits of being vegetarian, but taking meat off the shopping list will keep more money in the wallet.

A. As more people switch to a vegetarian diet, they may be happy to realize their monthly spending on groceries is going down.
B. You spend more money at the grocery store when you replace meat with meat alternatives like tofu and veggie burgers.
C. Eating less meat and eating more high-protein vegetables, like peas and edamame, will have a positive impact on blood pressure.

Lesson 4.2.4 Exercise: Pick the Concluding Sentence

Instructions: For each question, pick the concluding sentence that makes the most sense for the given prompt, claim, thesis statement, and topic sentence.

③ **Prompt:** What is the most important meal of the day? Explain your answer.

Claim: Breakfast is the most important meal of the day.

Thesis Statement: Breakfast is the most important meal of the day because it provides energy for activities and tasks throughout the rest of the day, replenishes vital nutrients, and kick-starts metabolism early in the morning.

Topic Sentence: Breakfast is an essential meal because it helps the body feel re-energized and ready to tackle the day.

A. Breakfast is vital because it helps stimulate one's metabolism.
B. As such, it is evident breakfast serves a vital role as the most important meal of the day. Without breakfast, having energy to do even the simplest of tasks would be difficult.
C. Having a smoothie for breakfast is a great way to consume vital nutrients.

④ **Prompt:** What is the best non-dairy milk alternative? Discuss your thoughts.

Claim: The best non-dairy milk alternative is oat milk.

Thesis Statement: The best non-dairy milk alternative is oat milk because it is creamier than most other alternatives, it has a great taste, and it is affordable.

Topic Sentence: No other non-dairy milk alternative can compare to the great taste of oat milk; it is delicious.

A. While some non-dairy milk alternatives, like cashew milk, are expensive, oat milk remains affordable for all.
B. Oat milk goes great in coffee, cereal, and even some soup recipes.
C. Oat milk's great taste makes it an indispensable item to have in the kitchen; it is a versatile non-dairy alternative and, simply put, delicious.

Lesson 4.2.5: Counterarguments

In Lesson 2.2, we went over clashing phrases. To recap, these are when your prompt contains a phrase with two words that oppose or *clash* with one another by asking you for **different** things.

If you have a clashing phrase in your prompt, you likely have *two supporting points* and *one opposing point*. You should not have three supporting points. Take a look at your outline.

Remember, opposing points are *reasons* that argue *against* your claim. They offer the *counterargument*. Counterarguments are important to show you are capable of understanding and addressing multiple opinions.

Even though a counterargument argues against the claim of your essay, it is often undermined by further analysis that ultimately supports your claim.

Your third body paragraph will serve as the *counterargument body paragraph*, and your opposing point will help you form the main idea of this paragraph.

A counterargument body paragraph follows the same core steps as a supporting body paragraph, which is what we have covered throughout Lesson 4.2 so far.

Before we go into detail about how to approach writing counterargument body paragraphs, let's first talk about why counterarguments are significant.

Why Make a Counterargument?

Let's face it: When you're trying to convince your reader to believe your argument, it seems a bit pointless to present another perspective, right? However, a counterargument strengthens your argument in two ways:

1. It shows you've considered multiple viewpoints but stuck with your argument because it has the most evidence to back it up.
2. If the reader doesn't agree with your argument, presenting a counterargument (which may be the same as your reader's viewpoint!) can show the reader why they should believe your argument over theirs.

How to Make a Counterargument Body Paragraph

To write a counterargument body paragraph, we follow four simple steps:

1. Form the opposing point into a topic sentence.
2. Give evidence for your counterargument.
3. Analyze your counterargument.
4. Add a concluding sentence.

You may recognize some of these steps from writing your supporting body paragraphs. The steps are exactly the same, except for a few tweaks we will show you in this lesson.

Just like your supporting argument, your counterargument should be well-thought-out and carefully explained. You'll need to write more than just a short sentence!

As mentioned before, if you look back over your outline, you'll find you already came up with an opposing point. This will serve as your counterargument! Let's use this as our example:

Prompt: Describe the advantages **and** disadvantages of hosting Thanksgiving dinner.

Claim: Hosting Thanksgiving dinner is great.

Thesis Statement: Although it is easy to get tired from prepping for Thanksgiving dinner all day, hosting Thanksgiving dinner is great because you are in charge of the menu and in control of the decor and activities.

Supporting Point 1: In charge of the menu for dinner

Supporting Point 2: In control of the decor and Thanksgiving activities

Opposing Point: Get tired easily from prepping for Thanksgiving all day

Step 1: Opposing Point to Topic Sentence

This step is simple. Take your opposing point and turn it into a full, coherent sentence that will express the main idea of your counterargument body paragraph.

You want to write your topic sentence as if you believe it yourself. Your reader will notice if you use language that suggests you don't believe it, such as "supposedly." They'll see you haven't really considered this viewpoint, and they won't want to accept yours. Here's an example of a topic sentence:

Topic Sentence: Hosting Thanksgiving can make you feel tired easily because of the sheer amount of prepping involved.

It may feel weird to write a topic sentence that refutes your claim, but we are presenting the counterargument here. In the coming steps, we will show you how to undermine and diminish the counterargument. Its significance will be minimized.

Step 2: Giving Evidence for Your Counterargument

Now, you need to provide evidence for your counterargument, just as you would for your supporting points.

Look at the bullet points in your outline for the body paragraph section that corresponds with your opposing point. In most cases, it would be Body Paragraph 3.

As we stated in Lesson 4.2.2 (Establishing Evidence), you don't need to transform all the bullet points you come up with in your outline to use as evidence in your essay.

Use as much or as little needed to prove the claim you made in the topic sentence. You might end up using all three bullet points, two bullet points, or just one! Use your best judgment. For the purposes of our example, we chose to transform all three bullet points into full sentences. Take a look at the example.

Body Paragraph 3 ➔ Opposing Point: Get tired easily from prepping Thanksgiving all day

- Cooking and prepping food all day makes you tired.
- Cleaning and prepping the whole house for Thanksgiving makes you tired.
- Getting ready and dressed after cooking and cleaning all day is tiring.

*Think about how this opposing point isn't a big deal. Despite this opposing point, why is your claim still true?

Evidence 1 ➔ When you spend all day cooking meticulous dishes for Thanksgiving, you're bound to get exhausted from standing, cutting vegetables, and prepping; it's physically demanding work, and your body will get tired.

Evidence 2 ➔ Not only that, but you also have to clean and prep the entire house when hosting Thanksgiving dinner. Cleaning an entire house is no small feat.

Evidence 3 ➔ Lastly, after all the exhausting cooking and cleaning, you still have to get yourself prepped, cleaned up, and dressed, which is the last thing anybody wants to do after hours of hard work and throbbing feet.

Step 3: Analyzing Your Counterargument

In the analysis step, you pick out the flaws of your counterargument. This is important because it shows the reader why they *shouldn't* hold this viewpoint. Your goal is to diminish the value of your *counterargument* and show why your *claim* is still true.

When looking for weaknesses in the counterargument, you can do one of the following:

1. Discredit the counterargument by bringing in lots of research that argues against the viewpoint.
2. Accept that the counterargument is true, but emphasize there is more evidence for your viewpoint (Matthews, 2020, p. 60).

Let's go through an example:

Prompt: Describe the advantages **and** disadvantages of hosting Thanksgiving dinner.

Claim: Hosting Thanksgiving dinner is great.

Opposing Point: Get tired easily from prepping for Thanksgiving all day

Analysis: Although hosting Thanksgiving dinner can be tiring, it is worth the trouble of preparation because you feel grateful for being able to provide a beautiful space and delicious food for all your loved ones. Seeing your family with glowing smiles and full tummies makes it worthwhile.

Can you see how the analysis example here acknowledges the counterargument is true? Can you also see how the following sentences in the analysis discredit and undermine the counterargument, ultimately reinforcing the original claim? It shows the reader why your viewpoint is valid, even when challenged by other perspectives.

Step 4: Concluding Sentence

Remember, to wrap up your body paragraph, you want a clear, concise sentence or two that tells the reader what the paragraph has proven. Don't forget to link it back to your thesis and original claim! Keep it simple.

Concluding Sentence: As such, it is clear hosting Thanksgiving dinner is great overall.

Putting It All Together

Now that we've gone through all four steps on how to write a counterargument body paragraph, let's put our whole paragraph together, so you can see what it looks like:

Counterargument Body Paragraph: {Topic Sentence} Hosting Thanksgiving can make you feel tired easily because of the sheer amount of prepping involved. **{Evidence}** When you spend all day cooking meticulous dishes for Thanksgiving, you're bound to get exhausted from standing, cutting vegetables, and prepping; it's physically demanding work, and your body will get tired. Not only that, but you also have to clean and prep the entire house when hosting Thanksgiving dinner. Cleaning an entire house is no small feat. Lastly, after all the exhausting cooking and cleaning, you still have to get yourself prepped, cleaned up, and dressed, which is the last thing anybody wants to do after hours of hard work and throbbing feet. **{Analysis}** Although hosting Thanksgiving dinner can be tiring, it is worth the trouble of preparation because you feel grateful for being able to provide a beautiful space and delicious food for all your loved ones. Seeing your family with glowing smiles and full tummies makes it worthwhile. **{Concluding Sentence}** As such, it is clear hosting Thanksgiving dinner is great overall.

Lesson 4.2.5 Exercise: Counterargument Craze

Instructions: First, consider a possible counterargument to the claim. Then, write a piece of analysis that undermines the value of the counterargument and ultimately supports the original claim.

1. **Claim:** Macs are better than PCs.

Possible Counterargument: _____

_____

Analysis: _____

_____

_____

_____

2. **Claim:** Parents should open a bank account for their children as soon as they can.

Possible Counterargument: _____

_____

Analysis: _____

_____

_____

_____

3. **Claim:** Physical education (PE) should be required in school.

Possible Counterargument: _____

_____

Analysis: _____

_____

_____

_____

4. **Your Claim:** _____

Your Possible Counterargument: _____

_____

Your Analysis: _____

_____

_____

End-of-Lesson 4.2 Exercise: Identify The Parts

Instructions: Underline the topic sentence, circle the evidence, draw a rectangle around the analysis, and draw a squiggly line under the concluding sentence for each body paragraph. Use the last question to write your own body paragraph(s).

① **Prompt: Why do people stereotype strangers? Explain your reasoning.**

Many individuals categorize the people and experiences in their life; stereotyping is just one way people categorize to bring order to the brain. Humans go through an automatic process of social categorization, which involves grouping people based on characteristics, such as race, age, ethnicity, religion, and gender (Weisman et al., 2014). By grouping individuals based on these characteristics, humans are easily able to organize the people they meet and the experiences they have in their brains. By simplifying social experiences, some individuals end up making assumptions about people that may not be true, which is akin to stereotyping. Though stereotyping a person based off a single trait is unfair, it is important to challenge the brain to stop making these assumptions.

② **Prompt: Describe whether you agree or disagree with the following statement: "You need money to be happy."**

Money can buy you a lot of things, but it can't buy you friendship. In fact, money does a good job of buying you the opposite of friendship because we tend to view our financial success through a selfish, individualistic lens, and less through a collectivistic lens (Gambini, 2020). Essentially, as we chase money, we can easily stray further away from the people we love. We focus so much of our time and energy on financial success that we ignore our friendships and social wellbeing. When thinking about what money can add to our lives, we should also consider what it might be taking away from us.

End-of-Lesson 4.2 Exercise: Identify The Parts

Instructions: Underline the topic sentence, circle the evidence, draw a rectangle around the analysis, and draw a squiggly line under the concluding sentence for each body paragraph. Use the last question to write your own body paragraph(s).

③ **Prompt: The legal age to drive in many U.S. states is 16. Discuss the positives and negatives of this law.**

16-year-olds are not fully developed mentally as they take the seat behind the steering wheel for the first time, which makes them more prone to getting into car accidents. During this adolescent phase, teenagers prefer to learn by doing rather than to learn in a traditional classroom setting (Katz, 2008). Yet, we cannot place full blame on teenage brains for the high accident rate. Driving education can be improved to prepare 16-year-olds more effectively, instead of being a generalized training that may not work for everyone (Walshe, 2017). Driving is unsafe for anyone if they are not trained properly; age should not be the only factor to consider when trying to make the roads safer.

④ **Prompt: Some people believe there's no point in reading fiction. Do you agree or disagree with this opinion?**

Creativity is of utmost importance for humans, and fictional literature is great for boosting creativity and imagination. Characters' experiences in fictional stories can influence how people feel about experiences in their own lives and can even inspire individuals to change their actions (Lo Basso, 2020). Reading about these characters' experiences can incite people to think bigger or think differently, as they realize there is more to life than they have seen. A work of fiction may start as an escape from real life, but it has the power to positively change lives.

End-of-Lesson 4.2 Exercise: Identify The Parts

Instructions: Underline the topic sentence, circle the evidence, draw a rectangle around the analysis, and draw a squiggly line under the concluding sentence for each body paragraph. Use the last question to write your own body paragraph(s).

⑤ **Your Prompt:** _____

_____

Your Body Paragraph(s): _____

_____

_____

_____

_____

_____

_____

_____

_____

_____

_____

_____

_____

_____

_____

_____

_____

Lesson 4.3: How to Write an Intriguing Conclusion

The conclusion is the last paragraph in your essay. It's the bottom bun of your handy hamburger.

Why do we include a conclusion?

- To bring together the essay's key points
- To show your thesis statement is valid
- To highlight why your reader should care about your argument
- To give your reader closure

Most students dread writing their conclusion—it feels like an impossible task. What they don't realize is they've already done all the hard work. The conclusion is just about tying up loose ends.

You can write an excellent conclusion in three simple steps we have divided into three different lessons:

4.3.1	Rephrase Your Thesis Statement
4.3.2	Wrap Up and Review Your Main Points
4.3.3	Tie It All Together and Close It

But before you write your conclusion, let's go over some things we don't want in the bottom bun!

Things to Avoid While Writing a Conclusion

Just like there are fundamental things you *should* include, there are some things you should steer clear of when writing your conclusion. Let's go through the most common ones.

1. **New Evidence**

   Although it's tempting to provide as much evidence for your topic sentences and thesis statement as possible, don't bring new evidence into your conclusion!

   Bringing in new evidence at the end of your essay will confuse the reader and leave these points underdeveloped. It's OK to include a sentence or two to explain the impact of the points you made earlier, but don't make new points altogether!

2. **Talking Your Way Out of Your Argument**

A common problem when writing essays occurs when the student writes a phrase at the end that lessens the importance of their argument. This could be something like "Although the evidence suggests . . . (your argument), you may not agree."

You've written four super-confident paragraphs on your essay prompt—don't sabotage yourself now! Be confident in your argument and stick to it.

3. **Corny Concluding Phrases**

Although phrases like "in conclusion" and "to conclude" work as well as any other concluding phrase, they're overused.

Your reader already knows they are at the end of the essay, so you don't need to remind them. If you've followed the structure set out in this guide, you won't need a corny concluding phrase!

4. **Repetition**

You're at the end. You've done a lot of work. At this point, it may seem unnecessary to rephrase your thesis statement and topic sentences, but it is important. If you simply *repeat* yourself, the repetition won't go unnoticed. Do not repeat.

Always, always, *rephrase*.

5. **Unimportant or Minor Details**

Over the course of your essay, you've made a lot of points. Some are more important and substantial than others. Stick to the big ideas in your conclusion and leave the little ones behind.

If you try to cover every individual point, you'll end up with a five-paragraph conclusion!

 Study Skill: Think about what the reader should remember once they have gone through your essay.

Lesson 4.3.1: Rephrase Your Thesis Statement

The first step in the conclusion is *rephrasing* your thesis statement. This notifies the reader your essay is coming to an end (Matthews, 2020, p. 67).

You may choose to bring in a strong phrase at the beginning to show your reader your thesis statement is valid. However, it is not always necessary. You can use any of the following at your discretion:

- It is without a doubt
- It is clear that
- The evidence demonstrates
- Evidently

*This is not an exhaustive list

You will take your original thesis statement and rewrite it using different words or phrases. It's OK to use more than one sentence to rephrase your thesis statement. The goal is to reinforce and reiterate the message of the thesis one last time to drive your conclusion home.

Original Thesis Statement: The three most important ways an individual can prepare for an earthquake are making a plan, identifying safe spaces indoors and outdoors, and having emergency supplies.

Rephrased Thesis Statement: Preparation is key when dealing with earthquakes. As such, formulating a plan, establishing safe spaces, and stockpiling emergency items can lessen the detrimental effects of an earthquake.

The process looks the same for rephrasing a thesis statement that includes an opposing point. Let's use our Thanksgiving dinner example.

Thesis Statement: Although it is easy to get tired from prepping for Thanksgiving dinner all day, hosting Thanksgiving dinner is great because you are in charge of the menu and in control of the decor and activities.

Rephrased Thesis Statement: It can't be denied hosting Thanksgiving dinner is a wonderful experience because you get to plan out all the activities, decorations, and menu to your liking, even though you may get exhausted from the preparation.

Lesson 4.3.1 Exercise: Ready to Rephrase?

Instructions: Here, you have six thesis statements. Rephrase these so they're conclusion ready! Take a look at the example for inspiration.

Example

Prompt: Pick an activity that you enjoy. Explain why the reader should try this activity.

Thesis Statement: You should try swimming because it is great for cardiovascular fitness, it is a non-weight-bearing exercise, and it helps you sleep.

Rephrased Thesis Statement: Swimming is an enjoyable, low-impact exercise that enhances sleep and improves fitness, so you should get out of your comfort zone and give it a shot.

① **Prompt:** Discuss the steps it takes to break a harmful habit.

Thesis Statement: There are several important steps required to successfully break a harmful habit, including identifying what you want to change, swapping the old habit for a new one, and allowing yourself to make mistakes.

Rephrased Thesis Statement: _____
_____
_____

② **Prompt:** Should paternity leave be as long as maternity leave? Argue for and against.

Thesis Statement: Although companies may suffer financially, paternity leave should be as long as maternity leave because it allows fathers to build a strong relationship with their child and provide support for the mothers after birth.

Rephrased Thesis Statement: _____
_____
_____

③ **Prompt:** Describe the key differences between cities and rural areas.

Thesis Statement: Cities and rural areas are starkly different because of their differing population sizes, their facilities, and the number of green spaces available.

Rephrased Thesis Statement: _____
_____
_____

Lesson 4.3.1 Exercise: Ready to Rephrase?

Instructions: Here, you have six thesis statements. Rephrase these so they're conclusion ready! Take a look at the example for inspiration.

④ **Prompt:** School uniforms are essential. Do you agree or disagree with this statement?

Thesis Statement: School uniforms should not be required because they don't benefit your learning, they suppress individuality, and they often cost a lot of money.

Rephrased Thesis Statement: _____
_____
_____
_____

⑤ **Prompt:** Explain why lying is a bad habit.

Thesis Statement: Lying is a bad habit because it can destroy trust, it upsets others, and it is morally wrong.

Rephrased Thesis Statement: _____
_____
_____
_____

⑥ **Your Prompt:** _____
_____
_____

Your Thesis Statement: _____
_____
_____

Your Rephrased Thesis Statement: _____
_____
_____
_____

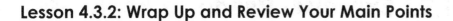

Lesson 4.3.2: Wrap Up and Review Your Main Points

The next step is to remind your reader of the main ideas from each body paragraph. You are not simply restating your main ideas and points here.

If you were trying to persuade your parents to buy unhealthy snacks, you would explain all the reasons why they should in a summary. This is exactly what you do here! You're going to summarize the main points from each body paragraph.

You want to connect all your ideas from your body paragraphs to show they work together to support your thesis statement and reinforce your claim. Keep your sentences brief, simple, and to the point. Your conclusion isn't meant to be a long paragraph.

And you can be flexible with the number of sentences you write. If you think you can summarize your main points into two coherent sentences, go for it! One sentence? The choice is in your hands.

Wrap Up and Review: While making a plan and having a strategy in place keeps you prepared and mitigates panic, identifying safe spaces allows you to respond quicker. And, of course, emergency supplies ensure you have everything you need, exactly when you need it.

If your essay includes a counterargument, you can easily include this in your conclusion. You can either bring it in at the beginning or the end of your paragraph! We'll be revisiting our Thanksgiving dinner example, so take a look.

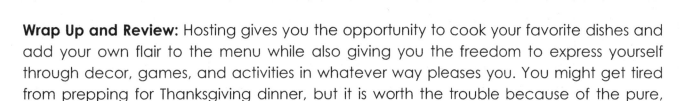

Wrap Up and Review: Hosting gives you the opportunity to cook your favorite dishes and add your own flair to the menu while also giving you the freedom to express yourself through decor, games, and activities in whatever way pleases you. You might get tired from prepping for Thanksgiving dinner, but it is worth the trouble because of the pure, unadulterated joy this holiday brings about.

OR

It's easy to get tired from prepping for Thanksgiving dinner, but it is worth the trouble because of the pure, unadulterated joy this holiday brings about. Additionally, hosting gives you the opportunity to cook your favorite dishes and add your own flair to the menu, while also giving you the freedom to express yourself through decor, games, and activities in whatever way pleases you.

Lesson 4.3.2 Exercise: Time to Wrap It Up

Instructions: Below, you have three sets of topic sentences. Use these topic sentences and summarize the main points. The last question is for your own essay.

1. **Prompt:** Explain in detail how someone can prepare for an earthquake.

Topic Sentence 1: Earthquakes can strike unexpectedly, so making a plan is an important step that an individual can take to prepare for one.

Topic Sentence 2: Establishing safe spaces ahead of time can be the difference between life and death when it comes to earthquakes.

Topic Sentence 3: When an earthquake hits, you can rest easy knowing you prepared an emergency supply kit.

Wrap Up and Review: _____
_____
_____
_____
_____

2. **Prompt:** Write an essay to persuade students to ride a bike to school instead of getting driven.

Topic Sentence 1: The physical health benefits of riding a bike should convince you to stop getting driven to school, if possible.

Topic Sentence 2: Starting the day by riding a bike, as opposed to sitting in a car, can have an immediate positive impact on your mental health.

Topic Sentence 3: It may seem hard to have a positive impact on the environment as just one student riding your bike to school, but many students riding their bike over the course of a school year will have an undeniable effect.

Wrap Up and Review: _____
_____
_____
_____
_____

Lesson 4.3.2 Exercise: Time to Wrap It Up

Instructions: Below, you have three sets of topic sentences. Use these topic sentences and summarize the main points. The last question is for your own essay.

3. **Prompt:** Is Google Docs better than Microsoft Word? Argue for and against.

Topic Sentence 1: Google Docs is better than Microsoft Word because it allows for easier collaboration.

Topic Sentence 2: Google Docs is better than Microsoft Word because you can see all of your edits.

Topic Sentence 3: When it comes to formatting tables and graphs, Microsoft Word may be the better option.

Wrap Up and Review: _____
_____
_____
_____
_____

4. **Your Prompt:** _____
_____

Topic Sentence 1: _____
_____

Topic Sentence 2: _____
_____

Topic Sentence 3: _____
_____

Wrap Up and Review: _____
_____
_____
_____
_____

Lesson 4.3.3: Tie It All Together and Close It

In this last step, you want to explain why everything you've talked about actually *matters*. You need to put your final thoughts and ideas together, so the reader leaves with a clear message and understands the importance of your essay. This will be your *closing statement.*

You need to choose your words wisely because, again, this is the last message the reader will be left with once the essay is over, and you have to make an impact!

If you're struggling with ideas, it might help to ask yourself these questions:

- How does this essay help people?
- Does it increase people's awareness of the overall topic?
- Are you presenting new ideas that haven't been talked about before? (This is a *no-no!*)
- Why is your essay important?
- What implications for the future does your essay have?
- What is the main message your reader should leave with (Matthews, 2020, p. 68)?

Here's a closing statement example that follows along with our earthquake essay!

Closing Statement: No matter how frightening earthquakes may be, we must take the proper measures to best prepare ourselves and diminish any adverse effects they may have on our lives.

The process is the same for writing a closing statement with an essay that includes a counterargument. Again, let's revisit our Thanksgiving dinner example.

Closing Statement: Thanksgiving is a celebration of gratitude, and if we have the means to host, we should be grateful for the bounty of food available to us, embrace the opportunity with grace, and remember to have fun.

Now that we have our closing statement, let's put the whole conclusion together.

Conclusion Without a Counterargument:

{Rephrased Thesis Statement} Preparation is key when dealing with earthquakes. As such, formulating a plan, establishing safe spaces, and stockpiling emergency items can lessen the detrimental effects of an earthquake. **{Wrap Up and Review}** While making a plan and having a strategy in place keeps you prepared and mitigates panic, identifying safe spaces allows you to respond quicker. And, of course, emergency supplies ensure you have everything you need, exactly when you need it. **{Closing Statement}** No matter how frightening earthquakes may be, we must take the proper measures to best prepare ourselves and diminish any adverse effects they may have on our lives.

Conclusion With a Counterargument:

{Rephrased Thesis Statement} It can't be denied hosting Thanksgiving dinner is a wonderful experience because you get to plan out all the activities, decorations, and menu to your liking, even though you may get exhausted from the preparation. **{Wrap Up and Review}** Hosting gives you the opportunity to cook your favorite dishes and add your own flair to the menu, while also giving you the freedom to express yourself through decor, games, and activities in whatever way pleases you. You might get tired from prepping for Thanksgiving dinner, but it is worth the trouble because of the pure, unadulterated joy this holiday brings about. **{Closing Statement}** Thanksgiving is a celebration of gratitude, and if we have the means to host, we should be grateful for the bounty of food available to us, embrace the opportunity with grace, and remember to have fun.

Lesson 4.3.3 Exercise: Fill in the Closing Statements

Instructions: Below are five concluding paragraphs without closing statements. Following the guidance from Lesson 4.3.3, fill in the closing statements. The first one has been done for you.

Example

Prompt: Explain in detail how someone can prepare for an earthquake.

Preparation is key when dealing with earthquakes. As such, formulating a plan, establishing safe spaces, and stockpiling emergency items can lessen the detrimental effects of an earthquake. Making a plan and having a strategy in place decreases stress and keeps you prepared, while safe spaces allow you to respond quicker and panic less. And, of course, emergency supplies ensure you have everything you need, exactly when you need it. **No matter how frightening earthquakes may be, we must take the proper measures to best prepare ourselves and diminish any adverse effects they may have on our lives.**

1. **Prompt:** Should carbohydrates be removed from the human diet? Explain your reasoning.

Carbohydrates are an essential component of the human diet. They are the body's main source of energy, and they're important for fiber intake. Removing them could result in nutrient deficiency. The body requires energy, fiber, and nutrients. Not getting a substantial supply of these vital dietary components can have long-term health implications (Behavioral Nutrition, 2020). _____

_____

_____

_____

Lesson 4.3.3 Exercise: Fill in the Closing Statements

Instructions: Below are five concluding paragraphs without closing statements. Following the guidance from Lesson 4.3.3, fill in the closing statements. The first one has been done for you.

2. **Prompt:** Describe the qualities that make someone trustworthy.

Trust can't be beaten; it's an integral part of any relationship. Trustworthiness can be broken down into consistency, loyalty, and honesty. A trustworthy person won't let you down. They'll stick to their word and never lie to you. They'll also remain loyal and truthful to you when others don't. _____

_____

_____

_____

3. **Prompt:** Should people use their phones and drive? Argue for or against.

There's no excuse for texting while driving. Sometimes there is an emergency, but you should avoid using your phone while driving because it reduces your attention on the road and increases the risk of a car accident. Although emergencies happen, using your phone while driving can cause severe injury, even death, as it makes crashes more likely. Because you're not paying as much attention, you increase the risk of harming yourself and others. _____

_____

_____

_____

4. **Your Prompt:** _____

Your Closing Statement: _____

_____

_____

_____

End-of-Lesson 4.3 Exercise: Identify The Parts

Instructions: Underline the rephrased thesis statement, circle the wrap up and review of main points, and draw a squiggly line under the closing statement for each conclusion. Write your own conclusion for the last question.

1 **Prompt: Why do people stereotype strangers? Explain your reasoning.**

Stereotyping is often not something we do on purpose; our brain wants to organize our experiences, it wants us to survive, and it wants us to avoid unexpected situations. It is easier to assume than to learn new information about people. By giving into our natural survival instinct, we tend to leave or avoid situations that may pose an unexpected threat to our safety. Though stereotyping is partially uncontrollable, we can take more control by learning more about people and being open to new experiences.

2 **Prompt: Describe whether you agree or disagree with the following statement: "You need money to be happy."**

Money is not some magical solution to everything in your life. It does not ensure long-term happiness, no matter what you buy, and it won't bring you closer to people. Having a lot of money makes things easier and convenient, but it is truly your mindset about money and life that will positively impact your happiness and your relationships. Money does have the power to greatly change your life, but if you value it too much or use it in the wrong ways, it can do a lot of damage.

End-of-Lesson 4.3 Exercise: Identify The Parts

Instructions: Underline the rephrased thesis statement, circle the wrap up and review of main points, and draw a squiggly line under the closing statement for each conclusion. Write your own conclusion for the last question.

③ **Prompt: The legal age to drive in many U.S. states is 16. Discuss the positives and negatives of this law.**

Despite the potential safety concerns of 16-year-olds being on the road, there is much benefit to them becoming drivers. Driving helps teens build life skills during a valuable time in their life, and it makes them more responsible for their transportation. Teens need to mature, and becoming drivers is one great way for them to take on more responsibilities, as long as it is done safely. With proper training, teens will be given the keys to becoming more independent and prepared to take on the rest of their lives.

④ **Prompt: Some people believe there's no point in reading fiction. Do you agree or disagree with this opinion?**

People are so often scared to take a break from the busyness of real life and jump into a fictional book, not realizing fictional works can improve inference and interpretation skills and expand creativity. Being a critical and creative thinker will bring you to places in life you might never have dreamed of, and that is why reading fiction can be so life changing. When we open our minds and our hearts to new ways of thinking and communicating, the line between fiction and nonfiction can become more blurred, and that is not always a bad thing.

End-of-Lesson 4.3 Exercise: Identify The Parts

Instructions: Underline the rephrased thesis statement, circle the wrap up and review of main points, and draw a squiggly line under the closing statement for each conclusion. Write your own conclusion for the last question.

(5) **Your Prompt:** _____

_____

Your Conclusion: _____

_____

_____

_____

_____

_____

_____

Essay Review

So, we've worked through every part of an essay. Let's put the earthquake example altogether and see how it looks! You'll notice a *transition sentence* has been added to the end of the first body paragraph, which was not included in the body paragraph examples in the previous lessons. We will explore what transitions are in the next lesson.

This essay example doesn't require a counterargument:

Prompt: Explain in detail how someone can prepare for an earthquake.

{Hook} An average of ten thousand people around the globe die from earthquakes every year (National Geographic, 2021). **{Background Information}** An earthquake is an aggressive trembling of the ground caused by movement of the Earth's crust, and descriptive records show they occurred as early as 1177 B.C. in China (Bolt, 2021; U.S. Department of the Interior, 2016). Fast-forwarding to modern times, in 2020 there were 938 earthquakes in Oklahoma, Texas, Louisiana, and New Mexico alone (Insurance Journal, 2021). Despite these common occurrences, many people are still ill-prepared for these life-threatening situations. **{Thesis Statement}** The three most important ways an individual can prepare for an earthquake are making a plan, identifying safe spaces indoors and outdoors, and having emergency supplies.

{Topic Sentence} Earthquakes can strike unexpectedly, so making a plan is an important step that an individual can take to prepare for one. **{Evidence}** Being properly equipped with a well-thought-out strategy and knowing what to do prevents scrambling around out of fear (FEMA, 2009). **{Analysis}** This will make your response more efficient and allow you to take cover quickly. If a carefully constructed plan helps you stay safe, the earthquake will have less of an impact. **{Concluding Sentence}** It is clear that developing a strategic plan eliminates many hazards during an earthquake and stops panic, and this makes it an effective method of preparation. Another effective method of preparation is identifying safe spaces indoors and outdoors.

{Topic Sentence} Establishing safe spaces ahead of time can be the difference between life and death when it comes to earthquakes. **{Evidence}** Pinpointing secure areas, such as under solid furniture, against an indoor wall, and away from glass can reduce unexpected struggle (OnHealth, 2008). In addition, knowing hazardous areas ahead of a crisis can reduce the likelihood of severe injury and even death (DIY Science, n.d.). **{Analysis}** It may seem like common sense to avoid dangerous areas and go to safe spaces, but it is easy to forget and panic in stressful situations. Think now so all you have to do later is act.

{Concluding Sentence} Recognizing safe spaces ensures you act quickly and steer clear of danger, making it an essential preparation method.

{Topic Sentence} Additionally, when an earthquake hits, you can rest easy knowing you prepared an emergency supply kit. **{Evidence}** Preparation of emergency supplies like food, water, a flashlight, and a whistle can ensure survival if you become trapped. Since injuries during an earthquake are common, and you may not have immediate access to a medical expert, a first aid kit is also imperative to have on hand. **{Analysis}** With a first aid kit, you can stabilize any injuries while help is sought. **{Concluding Sentence}** Hence, compiling an emergency supply kit is vital when preparing for an earthquake, as it lessens the impact of injury and increases the chances of survival.

{Rephrased Thesis Statement} Preparation is key when dealing with earthquakes. As such, formulating a plan, establishing safe spaces, and stockpiling emergency items can lessen the detrimental effects of an earthquake. **{Wrap Up and Review}** While making a plan and having a strategy in place keeps you prepared and mitigates panic, identifying safe spaces allows you to respond quicker. And, of course, emergency supplies ensure you have everything you need, exactly when you need it. **{Closing Statement}** No matter how frightening earthquakes may be, we must take the proper measures to best prepare ourselves and diminish any adverse effects they may have on our lives.

Now, let's take a look at our Thanksgiving dinner counterargument essay example. You'll notice phrases, such as "on the other hand," have been added in this example. These are called *transition words or phrases*, which we explore in the next lesson.

Prompt: Discuss the advantages and disadvantages of hosting Thanksgiving dinner.

{Hook}What holiday has people cooking up a whopping 46 million turkeys each year? Thanksgiving, of course (University of Illinois Extension, n.d.)! **{Background Information}** Thanksgiving dates back to 1621, when the Pilgrims celebrated a successful harvest and shared a feast with nearby Native American tribes, including the Wampanoag (Silverman, n.d.). Today, Thanksgiving is a celebration of gratitude and being thankful for family, friends, and good food. Most American households create elaborate dishes of juicy turkey, creamy mashed potatoes, and sweet apple pie for the notable and timeless Thanksgiving dinner. Thanksgiving dinner is a cornerstone of American culture, and many put forth their best effort to prepare for and host this holiday. **{Thesis Statement}** Although it is easy to get tired from prepping for Thanksgiving dinner all day, hosting Thanksgiving dinner is great because you are in charge of the menu and in control of the decor and activities.

{Topic Sentence} What's a better way to enjoy Thanksgiving dinner than to be in charge of the menu and host the dinner yourself? Nothing! **{Evidence}** Hosting Thanksgiving dinner is marvelous because you have the freedom to make all your favorite dishes. If you want to make something nontraditional, instead of the same old mashed potatoes and green beans, you can. In addition, you won't have to suffer through the day wondering what is being served and when it will be ready. You will know ahead of time and will likely get to taste everything during the course of the day. **{Analysis}** Much of the excitement surrounding Thanksgiving is attributed to the menu and classic dishes. So, when you are in charge of the menu, you are in charge of all the excitement and delighted taste buds, including your own! A menu you get to choose means a happy host and a happy holiday. **{Concluding Sentence}** That's what makes hosting Thanksgiving dinner so worthwhile and enjoyable.

{Topic Sentence} In addition, hosting Thanksgiving dinner is great because you get to pick the decor and all the wonderful activities. **{Evidence}** Everyone has a particular way they like to decorate the dinner table; hosting gives you the ability to add your own flair, whether glitzy, classy, minimal, or modern. If you want to go the extra mile and cover the house in papier-mâché turkeys, colorful leaves, and gourds, you have the option. Let's not forget you also get to decide all the activities because you're hosting. Scratch muddy flag football off the list and opt for some arts and craft activities instead if you like! **{Analysis}** The underlying theme here is that hosting Thanksgiving dinner gives you the capability and flexibility to customize the decor and activities the way you want. You won't have to deal with someone else's nagging input on the decorations you put out or the activities you choose. **{Concluding Sentence}** The appeal of hosting Thanksgiving dinner lies in the power to do what brings you joy, and that's what makes it so great!

{Topic Sentence} On the other hand, hosting Thanksgiving can make you feel tired easily because of the sheer amount of prepping involved. **{Evidence}** When you spend all day cooking meticulous dishes for Thanksgiving, you're bound to get exhausted from standing, cutting vegetables, and prepping. It's physically demanding work, and your body will get tired. Not only that, but you also have to clean and prep the entire house when hosting Thanksgiving dinner. Cleaning an entire house is no small feat. Lastly, after all the exhausting cooking and cleaning, you still have to get yourself prepped, cleaned up, and dressed, which is the last thing anybody wants to do after hours of hard work and throbbing feet. **{Analysis}** Although hosting Thanksgiving dinner can be tiring, it is worth the trouble of preparation because you feel grateful for being able to provide a beautiful space and delicious food for all your loved ones. Seeing your family with glowing smiles and full tummies makes it worthwhile. **{Concluding Sentence}** As such, it is clear that hosting Thanksgiving dinner is great overall.

{Rephrased Thesis Statement} It can't be denied hosting Thanksgiving dinner is a wonderful experience because you get to plan out all the activities, decorations, and menu to your liking, even though you may get exhausted from the preparation. **{Wrap Up and Review}** Hosting gives you the opportunity to cook your favorite dishes and add your own flair to the menu, while also giving you the freedom to express yourself through decor, games, and activities in whatever way pleases you. You might get tired from prepping for Thanksgiving dinner, but it is worth the trouble because of the pure, unadulterated joy this holiday brings about. **{Closing Statement}** Thanksgiving is a celebration of gratitude, and if we have the means to host, we should be grateful for the bounty of food available to us, embrace the opportunity with grace, and remember to have fun.

Lesson 4.4: Transitions

Transitions are words or phrases used to create a sense of flow to writing by bringing ideas together and connecting them.

They make writing clearer, so the reader can effortlessly read between ideas without paragraphs feeling jumpy and disorganized. Essentially, they help structure your writing. It's the proper use of transitional words and phrases that make the difference between muddled and well-ordered writing (Arquilevich, 1999, pp. 24–25).

Common Transition Words and Phrases

There are several types of transition words/phrases:

1.   Causal transitions: words or phrases suggesting one thing causes another
2.   Opposing transitions: words or phrases presenting an opposing idea
3.   Sequence transitions: words or phrases showing a sequence of events
4.   Agreement transitions: words or phrases showing one point supports another
5.   Summary transitions: words or phrases summing up your ideas

Let's look at examples of each and each type within a sentence.

Type of Transition	Common Transition Words	Example
Causal Transitions	Therefore Consequently Because So that If To Provided that	**Therefore**, it is important to remember to brush your teeth before bed.

Opposing Transitions	Although Whereas However Regardless Nonetheless Conversely While Alternatively On the other hand In spite of In contrast	Emily loves chocolate. **On the other hand**, Emma does not like chocolate.
Sequence Transitions	First/firstly First and foremost Second/secondly Third/thirdly Finally Lastly Subsequently To top it all off	**Firstly**, a shovel is an essential gardening tool because you can use it for transporting soil. **Secondly**, owning a shovel is crucial because it's useful for planting.
Agreement Transitions	Moreover For example Similarly Of course Furthermore Equally important Together with Additionally In addition	Footwear is important because it helps your feet heal. **Additionally**, footwear improves your posture.
Summary Transitions	On the whole In essence To summarize In summary Ultimately As shown above All things considered To sum up Altogether	**To summarize**, coffee is more popular in western countries, while tea is more widely used in eastern countries.

Transitions Within Paragraphs

The only way to gain an understanding of transitions and transitional phrases is to use them yourself. However, let's look at an example of a paragraph that utilizes transitions and transitional phrases in a few different ways first, so you can develop a familiarity with the concept:

Ever since I was a child, I always dreamt of going on vacation to Disney World and imagined what my perfect day would be like. **First**, *I would wake up in a king-size bed at the Polynesian Village Resort. My room would have a picturesque view.* **Second**, *I would get dressed and race down to the famous family-style restaurant, Ohana, to beat the crowds.* **Third**, *I would spend the day exploring Magic Kingdom with my family and going on all the rides imaginable. I would also eat all the whimsical snacks Disney World has to offer, like Dole Whip. It is worth mentioning,* **of course**, *that my perfect day would not be complete without an exquisite fine dining experience at the Be Our Guest Restaurant. I yearn to be immersed in its golden glory and romantic ambiance!* **To top it all off**, *I would spend the end of the day watching the magical Disney fireworks by the Cinderella castle. To me, this would be the perfect day of vacation at Disney World!*

Look at this example closely. What transition words or phrases do you see? There is a considerable amount of sequence transitions within the paragraph, such as "first," "second," and "third." These transition words help organize the sequence of events pertaining to the writer's perfect day of vacation in Disney World. Toward the end, we even see the transition phrase "to top it all off" being used to effortlessly tie in the last event of the day. As you may have noticed from the example, oftentimes when a transition word is used at the beginning of a sentence, it is followed by a comma. Make note of this.

Transition words or phrases are not limited to being used at the beginning of a sentence. Sometimes, they may appear in the middle of a sentence, if appropriate. Look at the placement of the transition phrase "of course." It appears in the middle of a sentence. Note that transition words or phrases that appear in the middle of a sentence usually have a comma before the word or phrase and after it as well (Arquilevich, 1999, p. 24).

Using transition words and phrases may seem scary and daunting if the concept is new to you, or if you're not confident in your abilities yet. Don't worry! With practice, you'll get the hang of it.

 Study Skill: You don't have to use a transition for every single sentence in your essay. In fact, it could look pretty weird if you did! Instead, choose the sentences you think need to be linked and bring in some transition words.

Transition Sentences Between Paragraphs

Transitions aren't only effective within a paragraph. We use transition sentences in between paragraphs as a way to flow from one main idea to another. These transition sentences link two consecutive paragraphs together and highlight how the paragraphs are related (Photinos, n.d.). This brings balance and fluidity to effective essay writing.

Now, you might be wondering, *Where do I put the transition? At the end of one paragraph? At the beginning of the next paragraph? In both places?* It's great to have questions like these because it means you are thinking about what makes most sense for your essay.

Transition sentences can go at the beginning of a paragraph to connect to the previous paragraph. Alternatively, transition sentences can go at the end of a paragraph to connect to the subsequent paragraph. Keep in mind there is no reason to include a transition sentence at the start of an introduction or the end of a conclusion.

To give you a better understanding, let's go through some examples. First, let's explore the beginning of a paragraph without a transition sentence and then with a transition sentence.

End of Body Paragraph 2: [...] The appeal of hosting Thanksgiving dinner lies in the power to do what brings you joy, and that's what makes it so great!

Beginning of Body Paragraph 3 Without Transition: Hosting Thanksgiving can make you feel tired easily because of the sheer amount of prepping involved. [...]

Beginning of Body Paragraph 3 With Transition: *On the other hand,* hosting Thanksgiving can make you feel tired easily because of the sheer amount of prepping involved. [...]

Without a transition sentence, there is no flow, and Body Paragraph 3 does not relate back to Body Paragraph 2 at all. It sounds a little choppy.

With a transition sentence, there is a bridge between the main ideas. We added the phrase "on the other hand," and this instantly created a transition sentence that linked Body Paragraph 3 back to Body Paragraph 2. This is what you want.

Take a closer look at the Thanksgiving essay in the Essay Review section if you want to see the full paragraphs for better context.

Next, let's look at an example where a transition sentence is used at the end of a paragraph to connect and lead into the subsequent paragraph:

End of Body Paragraph 2 With Transition: [...] The appeal of hosting Thanksgiving dinner lies in the power to do what brings you joy, and that's what makes it so great! *However, let's not forget that hosting Thanksgiving can also be exhausting.*

Beginning of Body Paragraph 3 Without Transition: Hosting Thanksgiving can make you feel tired easily because of the sheer amount of prepping involved. [...]

In this example, we added an entirely new sentence after the concluding sentence in Body Paragraph 2. We used the transition word "however" to oppose the main idea in Body Paragraph 2 and prepare the reader for a new point of view in Body Paragraph 3.

Sometimes, you can modify an existing sentence by adding a transition word or phrase to form a *transition sentence*, as shown in the first example. Or, you can add an entirely new sentence that serves as a transition sentence. It will likely include a transition word or phrase, as shown in the previous example.

Furthermore, the kind of transitions used between paragraphs is dependent on how the ideas in each paragraph are related. If the ideas support each other, transition words such as "similarly" and "additionally" can work well. If the ideas oppose each other, transition words or phrases such as "conversely," "however," or "on the other hand" would work.

After adding a transition, read a few sentences surrounding it. Does it seem like the transition improved the flow of ideas? Or does your writing no longer make sense? Sometimes, you need to be a little creative with your word choice to get that flow you are aiming for.

Lesson 4.4 Exercise: Fill in the Blank

Instructions: Circle the best transition word or phrase to fill in the blank. Then, check off what type of transition word or phrase you used (Miami Dade College, 2005).

1. Over 50 million U.S. citizens considered fishing a hobby in 2019 (Lange, 2020). It's safe to say fishing is a popular hobby. _____ fishing can be bad for the environment, it is a great hobby because it keeps you occupied.
A. Although
B. Because
C. Additionally
D. Lastly

Type of transition word: Causal   Opposing   Sequence   Agreement   Summary

2. Halloween is a wonderful time of year, when kids get to dress up, eat candy, and hang out with friends. _____, it beats out every other holiday.
A. Alternatively
B. Ultimately
C. Similarly
D. Thirdly

Type of transition word: Causal   Opposing   Sequence   Agreement   Summary

3. People should donate to charity because it supports other people. _____, it can be rewarding and bring a sense of fulfillment.
A. Yet
B. Meanwhile
C. Of course
D. Additionally

Type of transition word: Causal   Opposing   Sequence   Agreement   Summary

4. It is, _____, important to wash your hands regularly to maintain proper hygiene.
A. According to
B. Furthermore
C. Next
D. However

Type of transition word: Causal   Opposing   Sequence   Agreement   Summary

Lesson 4.4 Exercise: Fill in the Blank

Instructions: Circle the best transition word or phrase to fill in the blank. Then, check off what type of transition word or phrase you used (Miami Dade College, 2005).

5. The World Health Organization classifies processed meat, like hot dogs, as a Group 1 carcinogen. This is in the same group as cigarettes (2015). _____, humans should minimize the consumption of processed meat, or eliminate it altogether.
A. Consequently
B. Above all
C. Secondly
D. Because

Type of transition word: Causal   Opposing   Sequence   Agreement   Summary

6. _____, I like to start my day with cardiovascular exercise. Second, I fuel my body with a hardy breakfast.
A. Of course
B. Subsequently
C. First
D. On the whole

Type of transition word: Causal   Opposing   Sequence   Agreement   Summary

7. _____ Jeffrey prefers to eat filet mignon for lunch, Jenny likes to eat salmon with truffle oil potatoes instead.
A. Equally important
B. In essence
C. While
D. In spite of

Type of transition word: Causal   Opposing   Sequence   Agreement   Summary

8. _____ my brother is allergic to dairy, he cannot eat ice cream or pizza; these items upset his stomach.
A. All in all
B. To top it all off
C. Therefore
D. Because

Type of transition word: Causal   Opposing   Sequence   Agreement   Summary

Lesson 4.5: How to Come Up with an Effective Title for Your Essay

You might find it a bit bizarre we haven't mentioned the title until now. Well, there was a reason for this! You shouldn't write a title unless you know what your essay includes, and you don't know that for sure until you've written it!

So, writing a title should come *after* writing your essay.

Why Does a Title Matter?

The title is the first thing the reader sees. Though your audience might be someone who is going to read your essay anyway (e.g. your teacher, a classmate, your parent), it is still a good idea to put effort into writing an enticing title.

Your essay title determines whether or not your reader will read the rest of your essay or at least *want* to continue reading.

Your essay title is also a great chance to start presenting your viewpoint to the reader and to convince them to believe it too! Or, you can be more secretive with your title and keep your reader guessing. As you'll see in our example to come, you can make it work both ways.

Lastly, an effective title shows the reader you know what you're talking about. It highlights your knowledge and skill right from the get-go.

What Makes an Effective Title?

A title needs to be

- enticing,
- easy to follow,
- succinct, and
- relevant.

It needs to be interesting, much like your hook in the introductory paragraph, and easy to follow, or your reader won't continue reading!

It needs to be short and snappy, because the reader will get bored if it's too long and assume the rest of your essay is boring too.

Your title also needs to be relevant to the rest of your essay because what is the point of writing a title that has no relevance to your topic? It needs to show the reader what your essay is all about, or it will be misleading.

Writing Your Title

When coming up with a title, there are some factors to consider:

- Tone of your essay

If it's a very serious essay, you need a serious title. If it's a persuasive essay, you want a persuasive title, and so on.

- Audience

Just like the rest of your essay, your title needs to be tailored toward your audience!

- Essay prompt and thesis statement

Look back over your essay prompt and thesis statement. Remember how we talked about subject and command words? These are the keywords in your prompt—you can use these for your title!

- Your essay as a whole

Read through your whole essay. It'll remind you what your essay's key concepts are and will help you come up with an effective title.

There are two parts to an effective title:

1. A memorable phrase
2. An educational phrase

The memorable phrase grabs the reader's attention while the educational phrase informs the reader what your essay is all about. You usually do not *need* to have two parts to your title, but it gives you more options and more chances to draw your reader in (Wepler, 2013).

Let's see an example. First, we'll look at a title that needs some work. Then, we'll show you a new and improved one.

Prompt: Explain in detail how someone can prepare for an earthquake.

Subject Words: prepare for an earthquake

Command Word: explain

Needs Improvement: An Explanation as to Why It's Vitally Important to Prepare for an Earthquake if One Were to Arrive

New and Improved (you can't tell what the writer's exact viewpoint is yet): <u>Don't Be Shocked by Aftershock</u>: *A Detailed Explanation of How an Individual Should Prepare for an Earthquake*

New and Improved (you have some sense of the writer's viewpoint): <u>Protecting Yourself from Earthquakes</u>: *Why Waiting Is One of the Worst Things You Can Do*

The first example contains a lot of unnecessary words, making it long and boring to read. This won't entice the reader.

However, can you see how the first new and improved version is much better? The memorable phrase is underlined, and the educational phrase is italicized. We have also used the subject words and command words as inspiration. In the second new and improved version, we got a little more creative.

Lesson 4.5 Exercise: Title Time

Instructions: Based on the prompt, come up with a potential title for the essay! Since you don't have a thesis statement or any paragraphs to reference, you might want to brainstorm some ideas first before you jump right to the title.

← **Example**

Prompt: Discuss space travel since the year 2000.

Title: To Infinity, and Beyond! A Discussion on Space Exploration Since 2000

---

1. **Prompt:** Analyze the teenage perspective of climate change.

_____: An Analysis of David Attenborough's Impact on Teenagers

2. **Prompt:** Describe what you like about yourself.

_____: A Comprehensive Look at My Best Qualities

3. **Prompt:** Discuss what it means to be independent.

_____: The Importance of Independence

4. **Prompt:** What should you do in a meteor shower?
Quick, Take Cover! _____

5. **Prompt:** Analyze the effects of Covid-19 on small businesses.
Small Does Not Mean Insignificant: _____

6. **Prompt:** How can people become better communicators?
_____

7. **Prompt:** How does fiction affect children?
_____

8. **Try to craft a title for your own essay!**
Title: _____

Lesson 4.6: Citing and Referencing Your Work

In Chapter 2, we talked you through doing your research. We briefly touched upon referencing at that point, but we will go into more detail here.

You can present information from your sources in two ways:

1. In-text citations
2. References

We'll cover these soon. But first, why do we need to include them in the first place?

Why Citing and Referencing Sources Is Important

You wouldn't want someone else taking full credit for your hard work and original ideas, right? That's why, when taking information from sources, it's essential to reference them in your essay. It's important to give credit to those whose work you used. There are several reasons for this:

1. If you don't, you may be committing plagiarism.

   Plagiarism: presenting someone else's information or ideas as your own

   Plagiarism can get you into a lot of trouble, but don't be so scared of it that you don't use other people's ideas at all. You need to include information from your research to write a good essay—just don't pass these ideas off as your own!

2. It helps your reader find the source of the information.

   Your reader may want to look at the original source for extra information. Citing and referencing a source allows the reader to easily find it themselves!

3. It shows your reader you've done your research.

   When you include citations and references of your sources in your essay, it shows your reader you've really worked hard during the research stage and your information is reliable.

Study Skill: Try putting yourself in your reader's shoes. When they know where your information is coming from, they will trust you and be more likely to acknowledge your main ideas.

In-Text Citations

In-text citation: a mention of a source within the body of the writing

As you've worked your way through this guide, you may have noticed a name (or multiple names!) and a date in parentheses at the end of a sentence. It would have looked something like this:

(Smith, 2019)

This is a citation. There are three main citing styles:

1. MLA–Used for liberal arts and humanities (Purdue Writing Lab, n.d.-b)
2. Chicago Author-Date–Used for sciences (social, physical, and natural) (Western Oregon University, 2020)
3. APA–Used for social sciences and business (University of Arizona, 2021)

These three main citing styles have slightly different rules on how to cite and reference your sources. While the style you use depends on the sources you are citing, it may also be a decision your teacher ultimately makes. We are using APA in this guide, so our citations may look different than the ones in your work.

Let's break the different styles down, so they're easy to understand.

Citing Style	In-Text Citation
MLA	Sentence (Author last name + page number). Example for Reference with Consecutive Pages Impulsivity is defined as: "the inability to stop behavioral impulses and thoughts" (Chudasama 327-43). Example for Reference without Consecutive Pages Impulsivity is defined as "the inability to stop behavioral impulses and thoughts" (Chudasama 327, 333, 343).

Chicago Author-Date System	Sentence (Author last name + year of publication, page number).
	Example
	Impulsivity is defined as "the inability to stop behavioral impulses and thoughts" (Chudasama 2011, 327–43).
APA (Seventh Edition)	Sentence (Author last name, year of publication).
	Example
	Impulsivity is defined as "the inability to stop behavioral impulses and thoughts" (Chudasama, 2011).

References

References contain more information than your in-text citations, and they appear at the end of your essay in a "Works Cited" (MLA) or "References" (APA and Chicago) page. These pages are different from a "bibliography" you might find in a textbook or other source material. Bibliographies list sources that are not necessarily referenced within the document itself. Only sources you cite within your essay are included in the Works Cited or References page. Your reader will go to this page if they want to find out more about your sources and check you've referenced them correctly!

References can be tricky because you have to include different information for different types of sources.

Again, we've broken it down for you here, so it's easy to understand.

MLA Style	
Book Reference	Last Name, First Name of Author. *Book Title*. Publication City/Location, Publisher, Date of Publication.
	Example
	Dweck, Carol. *Mindset*. London, Robinson, 2017.

Website	Last Name, First Name of Author. "Title of Web Page." *Title of Website*, Publisher, Date published in day month year format, URL. Example Chudasama, Yogita. "Animal Models of Prefrontal-Executive Function." *PubMed*, Behavioral Neuroscience, June 2011, https://pubmed.ncbi.nlm.nih.gov/21639603/. *Note: This source did not have a specific publication day. Hence, the day has been omitted in the day month year format. Day month year format looks like this:* 8 June 2011.
Website with Missing Details	**No author** "Title of Web Page." *Title of Website*, Publisher, Date published in day month year format, URL. Example "Animal Models of Prefrontal-Executive Function." *PubMed*, Behavioral Neuroscience, June 2011, https://pubmed.ncbi.nlm.nih.gov/21639603/.
Personal Interview	Last Name, First Name of Interviewee. Personal Interview. Date conducted in day month year format. Example King, Stephen. Personal Interview. 15 May 2010.

Chicago Author-Date Style	
Book Reference	Last Name, First Name of Author. Year of Publication. *Book Title*. Publication Location: Publisher. Example Dweck, Carol. 2017. *Mindset*. London: Robinson.

Website	Last Name, First Name of Author. Date. "Title of Web Page." Website name. Last modified Month Day, Year. URL. Example Abraham, Micah. 2020. "How Anxiety Can Cause Forgetfulness." CalmClinic. Last modified October 10, 2020. https://www.calmclinic.com/anxiety/symptoms/forgetfulness.
Website with Missing Details	**No date** Last Name, First Name of Author. n.d. "Title of Web Page." Name of Website. Accessed Month Day, Year. URL Example Abraham, Micah. n.d. "How Anxiety Can Cause Forgetfulness." CalmClinic. Accessed October 28, 2021. https://www.calmclinic.com/anxiety/symptoms/forgetfulness.
Personal Interview	Personal interviews aren't included in the References in Chicago author-date style. The circumstances of the personal interview should be included in the text.

APA Style (Seventh Edition)	
Book Reference	Last Name, First and/or Middle Initial of Author. (Year of Publication). *Title of book*. Publisher. Example Dweck, C. (2017). *Mindset*. Robinson.
Website	Last Name, First and/or Middle Initial of Author. (Year of Publication, Month Day). *Title of page*. Site name. URL Example Curtis, S. (2019, August 6). *How growth mindset makes for better student writing*. EducationWeek. https://www.edweek.org/teaching-learning/opinion-how-growth-mindset-makes-for-better-student-writing/2019/08

Website with Missing Details	**No author** *Title of page.* (Year of Publication, Month, Day). Site name. Retrieved Month Day, Year, from URL <u>Example</u> *How to use the rule of three to create better marketing content.* (2014, October 14). Gigasavvy. Retrieved October 28, 2021, from https://www.gigasavvy.com/how-to-use-the-rule-of-three-to-create-better-marketing-content/ **No date** Last Name, First and/or Middle Initial of Author. (n.d.). *Title of page.* Site name. URL *The n.d. stands for "no date."* <u>Example</u> Gardiner, J. (n.d.). *Tapping into the subconscious.* Oxford Open Learning. https://www.oxfordhomeschooling.co.uk/blog/tapping-into-the-subconscious/
Personal Interview	Personal interviews aren't included in the References in APA style. The circumstances of the personal interview should be included in the text.

It's important to mention while this lesson provides sufficient information to have a preliminary understanding of in-text citations and references, there is much that has not been covered. It is impossible to fit every scenario for all existing citation styles within this book. If you are looking for a more in-depth and comprehensive explanation of citations and references, you may want to refer to specific citation style guides to supplement your learning.

Lesson 4.6 Exercise: Choose the Reference

Instructions: Below, you're given 3 types of references for each citation style, with two options for each reference. Choose which one is correct. There are two trick questions hidden in here somewhere —keep a lookout!

MLA:

Book

1 **A.** Shakespeare, W. (1993). *Romeo and Juliet*, Dover Publications, New York.

B. Shakespeare, William. *Romeo and Juliet*. New York, Dover Publications, 1993.

Website

2 **A.** Pickrell, John. "Top 10: Controversial Pieces of Evidence for Alien Life." *New Scientist*, 4 September 2006, https://www.newscientist.com/article/dn9943-top-10-controversial-pieces-of-evidence-for-alien-life/

B. Pickrell J. "Top 10: Controversial Pieces of Evidence for Alien Life," *New Scientist*. 4 September 2006.

Personal Interview

3 **A.** Johnson, David. Personal Interview. 20 August 2011.

B. Johnson, David, 20 August 2011. Personal Interview.

Chicago Author-Date:

Book

4 **A.** Zusak, Markus. *The Book Thief*. Great Britain: Transworld Publishers, 2005.

B. Zusak, Markus. 2005. *The Book Thief*. Great Britain: Transworld Publishers.

Website

5 **A.** Caulfield, Jack. "A Step-by-Step Guide to the Writing Process," Scribbr, April 24, 2020 https://www.scribbr.com/academic-writing/writing-process/.

B. Caulfield, Jack. 2020. "A Step-by-Step Guide to the Writing Process." Scribbr. Last modified April 24, 2020 https://www.scribbr.com/academic-writing/writing-process/.

Lesson 4.6 Exercise: Choose the Reference

Instructions: Below, you're given 3 types of references for each citation style, with two options for each reference. Choose which one is correct. There are two trick questions hidden in here somewhere —keep a lookout!

Personal Interview

⑥ **A.** Robert Brown. Interview by Sarah Martin. Personal Interview. 11 January 2001.

B. Brown, Robert. Interview by Sarah Martin. Personal Interview. Louisiana City Hall, 11 January 2001.

APA:

⑦ **Book**

A. Obama, Barack. Dreams From My Father. New York: Times Books. 1995.

B. Obama, B. (1995). *Dreams From My Father*. Times Books.

⑧ **Website**

A. Taylor, J. (2013, April 2). Has America become too competitive? *Psychology Today*. https://www.psychologytoday.com/gb/blog/the-power-prime/201304/has-america-become-too-competitive

B. Taylor, J. (2013). *Has America Become Too Competitive?* Psychology Today. Retrieved from https://www.psychologytoday.com/gb/blog/the-power-prime/201304/has-america-become-too-competitive

⑨ **Personal Interview**

A. Winfrey, Oprah. Personal interview. 17 November 2012.

B. Winfrey, Oprah. Personal interview. November, 17 2012.

Chapter 4 Comprehension Quiz

Instructions: Circle the best answer.

1. **What should your introduction <u>always</u> include?**
   a. A hook
   b. Background information
   c. Your thesis statement
   d. All of the above

2. **What is a hook?**
   a. A concluding sentence
   b. A point that supports your thesis statement
   c. The first sentence of your essay that grabs the reader's attention
   d. A sentence that transitions smoothly into the next paragraph

3. **What is the purpose of background information?**
   a. To add context to your introductory paragraph
   b. To analyze your evidence
   c. To explain your supporting point
   d. To conclude your essay

4. **What are the four elements of a body paragraph**
   a. Hook, background information, evidence, and thesis statement
   b. Topic sentence, evidence, analysis, and concluding sentence
   c. Background information, evidence, analysis, and concluding sentence
   d. Topic sentence, hook, background information, and analysis

5. **What is the point of establishing evidence?**
   a. It shows the connection between the evidence and the topic sentence.
   b. It gives proof to support your topic sentence.
   c. It concludes the essay.
   d. It hooks the reader.

Chapter 4 Comprehension Quiz

Instructions: Circle the best answer.

6. **One way to present analysis is through interpretation. What does this mean?**
   a. Adding detail to your supporting information
   b. Making it clear what your hook means
   c. Describing what your supporting information means in reference to your thesis statement
   d. Making a comment on the information you've presented

7. **What are the two main goals when concluding a body paragraph?**
   a. Summarize the main idea of your essay and link back to your hook.
   b. Summarize the main idea of your paragraph and link back to your thesis statement.
   c. Make additional points that you forgot to mention.
   d. Summarize the main ideas of your essay and give your reader closure.

8. **What does it mean to "rephrase" your thesis statement?**
   a. Keep it exactly the same.
   b. Create a new, unrelated sentence.
   c. Change one word.
   d. Change the sentence, so it uses different words but has the same meaning.

9. **What are the two components of an effective title?**
   a. A memorable phrase
   b. An educational phrase
   c. A concluding sentence
   d. Both A and B

10. **Why is it important to cite and reference sources in your essay?**
   a. If you don't, you may be committing plagiarism.
   b. It shows the reader you've done your research.
   c. It helps the reader find the source.
   d. All of the above

STEP 4

Polish and Shine

STEP 4

CHAPTER 5

Cleaning Up Your Essay

There's no doubt by now you've written a killer essay. However, it's bound to need a few tweaks here and there; every first draft does!

This chapter is all about cleaning up your essay, and it's part of Step 4: Polish and Shine.

We'll make some changes to content structure, fix any grammatical mistakes, and make sure you're using the best language to make your essay really stand out. The three lessons we cover are also the three steps required for this process:

5.1.   Revising
5.2.   Editing
5.3.   Proofreading

Plenty of people get these techniques mixed up. It's an easy mistake to make! By taking you through each step individually, we'll clear up any confusion you have.

Now, when it comes to cleaning up your essay, timing is key. You're not alone if you think the best time to get rid of those grammatical errors is while you're writing your essay.

When you're writing your first draft, it's super easy to get carried away editing your work. But this actually stops the flow of your writing. Of course, if you see a typo, it's only natural to correct it midway through writing a sentence, but try not to make big edits during the drafting stage (Arquilevich, 1999, pp. 33–35)!

Now that you know *when* to make the changes, here are some handy tips and tricks to help you out before we get into the nitty-gritty.

Take a Breather

Take a breather between writing your first draft and revising, editing, and proofreading your essay.

You may want to whiz through your essay as quickly as possible, but taking a break can help you clear your mind and come back with a fresh set of eyes.

Imagine You're the Audience

During the Polish and Shine step, you'll read your essay many times over. You may be so busy focusing on your essay's overall idea, its flow, and spelling and punctuation mistakes that it can be really easy to forget about your audience.

Take some time to read through your essay, imagining you are your intended audience. Think about whether there are parts of your essay that may be unclear to someone who isn't familiar with the topic.

Have you used the right tone? Remember, when we talked about identifying your audience, we talked about tone. If you're writing for your teacher, you'll need a formal tone. If you're writing for your classmates, maybe an informal tone will be just fine.

Print Out a Paper Copy

Revising, editing, and proofreading are all easier when you're working on a paper copy of your essay rather than straight off your computer document.

You can highlight and scribble all over the paper copy, and then type up the changes you've made. If you've handwritten your first draft, you could type it up, print it, *then* write all over it.

These tips, along with those in the lessons, will ensure you finish with a flawless and engaging essay!

Lesson 5.1: Revising

This is the first step after you've finished your first draft. The revision stage is where you analyze your essay as a whole. When revising, ask yourself the following:

- Does my essay support my thesis statement?
- Does my essay fit the purpose I set for it?
- Does the essay flow nicely with a structure that works well?

This stage isn't about checking for typos or getting into the weeds of every sentence. It's about looking at big problems, checking the essay as a whole, and looking at whether it answers the prompt fully.

Focus on the big things—don't get bogged down in the little issues!

Let's go through the two easy steps required to revise your essay effectively!

Step 1: Review

So, you've come back to your essay after taking a break. You may notice a few errors suddenly popping out you hadn't noticed before! That's OK.

Read your entire essay again. Try reading it aloud; this can really make those big issues jump out.

To thoroughly check over your essay, there are several things to think about. We've included a to-do list to follow. Think about each of these points before making any changes.

Revising My Essay To-Do List	
Structure	
My essay has a title.	
My paragraphs are roughly the same size.	
My paragraphs are in the right order.	
Introductory Paragraph	

My introductory paragraph includes an engaging "hook."	
My introductory paragraph includes background information for context.	
My thesis statement includes three supporting points.	
Body Paragraphs	
My body paragraphs contain a strong, coherent topic sentence. *Remember, your topic sentence can be more than one sentence.	
Body Paragraph 1 contains a topic sentence that matches a supporting point in my thesis statement.	
Body Paragraph 2 contains a topic sentence that matches a supporting point in my thesis statement.	
Body Paragraph 3 contains a topic sentence that matches a supporting point in my thesis statement.	
I've provided evidence in each paragraph.	
My evidence is analyzed fully, so the reader can see how it relates to the thesis statement.	
Each body paragraph includes a strong, coherent concluding sentence.	
Conclusion	
My conclusion includes my rephrased thesis statement.	
My conclusion brings together all my main points and ties them together.	

My conclusion includes a closing statement.	
Citations	
I have cited all my information correctly with in-text citations.	
I have included a works cited/reference page with correctly formatted citations.	
Flow	
My essay has a nice flow overall with the proper use of transitions and transitional phrases.	
Only complete these extra points if your prompt contains a clashing phrase.	
My thesis statement contains an opposing point.	
Body Paragraph 3 contains a topic sentence that matches the opposing point in my thesis statement.	
I have provided evidence for my counterargument.	
I have picked out the flaws in my counterargument.	

Step 2: Make Changes

Before making any changes, save a new copy under a different title if you've typed your essay on a computer. It could be "My Essay–Revised."

Work through each point on the to-do list. Identify whether you've met each criterion, and if you haven't, make changes, so you can tick off the point on the list.

This list goes through your paragraphs in order. You can work through your essay like this, or you can focus on the areas that require the most changes first. It's up to you!

And if you find sentences that are completely unnecessary, cut them out!

Lesson 5.1 Exercise: Does It Relate?

Instructions: Assess whether the topic sentence makes sense according to its corresponding thesis statement. Would it lead to a body paragraph that helps prove the thesis?

1. **Thesis Statement:** It's important to own an umbrella because it protects you from the rain, shields you from the sun, and helps prevent illness caused by getting wet.

Topic Sentence: Umbrellas are essential items to carry because they can shield you from the sun.

Does the topic sentence relate to the thesis?
Yes
No

2. **Thesis Statement:** Chocolate mousse is the perfect dessert because it is light, velvety, and creamy in texture.

Topic Sentence: Ice cream is better than chocolate mousse because it's the perfect summer dessert.

Does the topic sentence relate to the thesis?
Yes
No

3. **Thesis Statement:** Antioxidants are good for you because they help prevent disease, reduce inflammation in the body, and protect cells from damage caused by free radicals (Brennan, 2020).

Topic Sentence: Pomegranates are an excellent source of antioxidants, and they're delicious, too!

Does the topic sentence relate to the thesis?
Yes
No

Lesson 5.1 Exercise: Does It Relate?

Instructions: Assess whether the topic sentence makes sense according to its corresponding thesis statement. Would it lead to a body paragraph that helps prove the thesis? Circle the best answer.

4. **Thesis Statement:** Benjamin Franklin is important to American history because he helped draft the Declaration of Independence, served as the U.S. representative in France during the American Revolution, and made significant contributions to science (History.com, 2022).

Topic Sentence: Benjamin Franklin's contributions to science made him an important figure in U.S. history.

Does the topic sentence relate to the thesis?
Yes
No

5. **Thesis Statement:** Socks should be worn with shoes because they absorb sweat and reduce rubbing. However, some people with sensory difficulties become overwhelmed by the feel of socks.

Topic Sentence: Socks are not essential because some people are unable to wear them due to sensory difficulties.

Does the topic sentence relate to the thesis?
Yes
No

Lesson 5.1 Exercise: Check the Language

Instructions: Underline the first few words of each sentence in the included body paragraphs. Then, answer the questions that follow.

1. Prompt: Describe the impact burns have on the body.

Burns can negatively impact the body by causing scars. Thermal burns increase the skin's temperature and can cause skin tissue to die. Radiation burns also cause scars, as they can burn away layers of skin (University of Rochester Medical Center, n.d.). Scars can have an effect on the sufferer's mental health, which has a further impact. Therefore, scars have serious consequences because they cause permanent damage to the skin and tissue and can affect mental health.

Is the language consistent? Explain your answer.

_____
_____
_____

Does the language flow nicely? Explain your answer.

_____
_____
_____

Give one word to describe the topic of the paragraph.

_____

2. Prompt: Explain the importance of sunlight in the process of photosynthesis.

The cycle of photosynthesis is not able to start without energy from the sun. Water is also essential because it reacts with carbon dioxide forming glucose, which the plant uses for energy. The water molecules are released into the atmosphere, which animals breathe in. Water plays a vital role in chlorophyll activation, which creates the green color in plants (Vedantu, 2021). It is clear sunlight is an important component in the process of photosynthesis. Carbon dioxide is another key component.

Is the language consistent? Explain your answer.

_____
_____
_____

Does the language flow nicely? Explain your answer.

_____
_____
_____

Give one word to describe the topic of the paragraph.

_____

Lesson 5.1 Exercise: Check the Language

Instructions: Underline the first few words of each sentence in the included body paragraphs. Then, answer the questions that follow.

3. **Prompt: Is there a book you would recommend to anyone? Explain your choice.**

I would recommend *Harry Potter and the Sorcerer's Stone* by J. K. Rowling to anyone because it is engaging for everyone. Harry Potter and the Sorcerer's Stone is the most popular book of the series, with 500 million copies sold worldwide (Pottermore, 2018). This book interests people of all ages because it contains important life lessons about friendships, empathy, and bravery. With female and male main characters, this book is inspiring for both genders. *Harry Potter and the Sorcerer's Stone* is a great book to recommend to anyone because anyone can relate to it. I would also recommend the book because it can provide an escape from reality.

Is the language consistent? Explain your answer.

_____

_____

_____

Does the language flow nicely? Explain your answer.

_____

_____

_____

Give one word to describe the topic of the paragraph.

_____

Lesson 5.2: Editing

Editing focuses on style and consistency. You're no longer looking at the whole idea of your essay but rather how you're presenting your idea to the reader.

Just like revising, it's not about changing one or two words or removing a couple of sentences. It's about adapting your essay so it's well-written and easy to read. It's also about picking up on things you may have missed in the revising process because, come on, you can't notice everything all the time (Arquilevich, 1999, pp. 33–35)!

Study Skill: Just like in the revising step, reading your essay aloud can really help here! Keep an eye out for unnecessary words and sentences that don't flow correctly.

Cutting Out Unnecessary Words/Phrases

It's not always easy knowing which words or phrases are necessary and which are just fluff. Of course, you need the vital parts of each paragraph, but are they concise? Or are there too many unneeded words in the mix?

When writing is concise, it showcases your idea in a clear manner, so it's easy for the reader to identify and understand. It uses the fewest words possible to convey the idea without making it difficult to comprehend.

Making your essay succinct is one way to prove to your reader you haven't just handed them your first draft.

Concise writing has two main enemies:

1. Wordy sentences
2. Repetition

Let's discuss these *enemies* in further detail.

Wordy Sentences

A wordy sentence is one that's too long because it contains unnecessary words. Let's look at an example.

Wordy Sentence: Indoor plants could be thought of as a great alternative for the type of people who are not able to have a garden.

Concise Sentence: Indoor plants are a great alternative for people who cannot have a garden.

Can you see how the meaning is the same, but the sentence is much shorter?

Here are some phrases that make sentences unnecessarily wordy:

Wordy Phrase	Concise Phrase/Word
At this current moment in time	Currently
Due to the fact that	Because
Have the ability to	Be able to OR can
Not able to	Unable to OR cannot
In the event that	If
What's more	Additionally
In order to	To

Can you spot any of these examples in your essay? You know what to do!

Repetition

No reader wants to read the same thing over and over and over again. You got bored just reading that sentence, right?

Of course, there will be some phrases that need to be repeated, such as your thesis statement and your ideas for each body paragraph.

Often, when you're writing, it's easy to get carried away and put additional words in a sentence which carry the same meaning. Here's an example:

Repetitive Sentence: Renewable energy and fossil fuels have been competing against each other for a significant period of time.

Concise Sentence: Renewable energy and fossil fuels have competed for a long time.

Can you see how "against each other" isn't necessary because the word "competing" already tells us they're against each other? Additionally, the long, drawn-out phrase "significant period of time" can be replaced with "long time."

Let's look at some more examples.

Repetitive Phrases	Concise Words
Ask the question	Ask
Brief summary	Summary
First of all	Firstly
Informative facts	Facts
Scientific experts	Scientists or Experts

Again, look through your essay and see what you can find!

Here's an editing to-do list to make sure you've covered everything!

Editing To-Do List	
Are my ideas clear?	
Are my ideas easy to understand for the reader?	
Are there any sections or sentences that may be confusing to my reader?	
Do I stick to my ideas or bring in unrelated points?	
Does my language sound too casual/informal?	
Have I used the best vocabulary? Can my wording be more precise?	
Do I have wordy sentences?	
Can I simplify repetitive phrases?	
Does each word in every sentence serve a purpose? Does each word inform the reader and make each sentence easy to understand and read?	

Lesson 5.2 Exercise: Are You Being Clear?

Instructions: Below, there is a list of sentences. Take a look at each sentence and answer the questions that follow. Provide an alternative for each if necessary. Once you've worked through the sentences in this exercise, repeat the process with your own essay sentences.

1. It is often the case that cats and dogs don't get on with each other.

Read the sentence out loud. Is it clear? Does it make sense? Does the language sound awkward? Explain your answer.

_____

_____

_____

Are there better words that can be used while keeping the same meaning?

_____

_____

_____

Rewrite the sentence if you think it's necessary.

_____

_____

2. At this current moment in time, more people watch TV than play video games.

Read the sentence out loud. Is it clear? Does it make sense? Does the language sound awkward? Explain your answer.

_____

_____

_____

Are there better words that can be used while keeping the same meaning?

_____

_____

_____

Rewrite the sentence if you think it's necessary.

_____

_____

Lesson 5.2 Exercise: Are You Being Clear?

Instructions: Below, there is a list of sentences. Take a look at each sentence and answer the questions that follow. Provide an alternative for each if necessary. Once you've worked through the sentences in this exercise, repeat the process with your own essay sentences.

3. You can't not agree with people when they are able to prove that you are wrong.

Read the sentence out loud. Is it clear? Does it make sense? Does the language sound awkward? Explain your answer.

_____
_____
_____

Are there better words that can be used while keeping the same meaning?

_____
_____
_____

Rewrite the sentence if you think it's necessary.

_____
_____

4. Each and every time you think about a past memory, you activate a certain part of your brain.

Read the sentence out loud. Is it clear? Does it make sense? Does the language sound awkward? Explain your answer.

_____
_____
_____

Are there better words that can be used while keeping the same meaning?

_____
_____
_____

Rewrite the sentence if you think it's necessary.

_____
_____

Lesson 5.3: Proofreading

Proofreading is the final step in cleaning up your essay and the last thing you do before you hit the submit button!

Once you've checked your essay as a whole and reviewed the individual sentences, it's time to check the small stuff, including spelling, grammar, and punctuation errors!

Don't proofread until you have finished revising and editing. Otherwise, you'll be proofreading text you may end up changing or removing!

 Study Skill: Print your essay out and use the proofreader's annotating table to pick out the errors.

Handy Proofreading Tips

1. Reading your sentences out loud will make spelling errors pop out at you.
2. Go through your essay at least twice. You'll be surprised by how much you miss the first time around!
3. After you've checked through it, ask a friend or family member to check it as well! It's great to get another set of eyes on it.
4. You can use spell checkers and grammar checkers, but don't rely on them. They are no replacement for your own eyes and brain.

Professional editors use a set of symbols known as "proofreader's marks." Just like the professionals, you can use these when proofreading your essay.

Here's the proofreader's annotating table:

Proofreader's Sign	What Does It Mean?	Example
∧	Add a word	She was scared of dropping ∧the ball.
≡	Capitalize	who cares what they think, anyway?
⁄	Make lowercase	Sally said, "Becky, go Home."
SP	Spelling mistake	Mars is a plante in space.
¶	Start a new paragraph	In addition to making you unproductive, clutter can also negatively affect your mood ¶A messy room can worsen sad feelings . . .
#	Add a space	He wouldn't letme help him.
⋏	Add a comma	You need to eat⋏drink, and sleep.
⊙	Add a period	The dog was barking⊙
ⱽ	Add an apostrophe	Peters alarm clock was going off.
ℓ	Remove	The dog wouldn't stop stop barking.
∽	Swap words	It something was she had to do.
RO	Run-on sentence	One key component of a healthy relationship is honesty, and it's also great when two people share a sense of humor, RO but independence is also important and should not be sacrificed or there might be feelings of resentment RO and that is something both people should avoid.
ⱽ ⱽ	Add quotation marks	Dogs are man's best friend, she said.

(Arquilevich, 1999, pp. 35)

189

Just like with revising and editing, here's a proofreading to-do list, so you can make sure you've covered everything before submitting your essay:

Proofreading To-Do List	
With fresh eyes, have I checked my whole essay for spelling, capitalization, and punctuation errors?	
Do any of my sentences appear wordy or awkward?	
Have I read my essay out loud at least twice, checking for grammatical errors?	
Did I use the proofreader's annotating table to proofread my essay?	
Has a family member or friend checked over my essay, too?	
Do I have a finalized, proofread version of my essay?	

Lesson 5.3 Exercise: Find the Mistakes

Instructions: Using the proofreader's annotating table, proofread the sentences. Check for errors in spelling, punctuation, and formatting. Sentences 1-5 have one mistake, and Sentences 6-10 have two!

Find ONE mistake in each sentence.

1. Omega-3 lowers blood pressure looks after the heart, and reduces the likelihood of heart disease (Mayo Clinic, n.d.).

2. eating breakfast will give you energy for the rest of the day.

3. Birds migrate across world the for winter.

4. She screamed "don't do that," as he ran away.

5. ividince show there is a buildup of magma in a volcano before it erupts.

Find TWO mistakes in each sentence.

6. The distance between the the two stations were three miles.

7. she spent her day swimming in the sea

8. Samanthas dad had runned out of patience.

9. alex loves to Sell homemade scarves.

10. The dog barked at squirrel running aroundoutside.

Lesson 5.3 Exercise: Mark It Up

Instructions: Here's a passage with lots of mistakes! Using the proofreader's marks, correct the passage.

My first experince with kindness was my mom scoopin me up as a child. I had tumbled over while sprinting an ice cream truck. She cradled me in her arm and sang a lullaby softly while gently rooking me back forth. I knew in that moment what kindness warmth and love felt like Since then I have looked for for kindness in other people. However there's nothing quite like the love of your parents/guardians; it's unconditnal.

My second experience with kindness was from a freind. My cat had missing that weekend. I still remember the intense anxiety I felt I was distracted in school and, quiet when with my friends. One friend, Melissa, took me Aside and checked up on me, saying she had noticed was quiet. I told her about my cat. It's normal for cats to go missing for a couple of days, she said. Shereassured me that he would return soon. This act of Kindness, melissa noticing my frantic behavior and checking up on me, is something i'll always remember.

Chapter 5 Comprehension Quiz

Instructions: Circle the best answer.

1. **What are the three parts in the Polish and Shine step of essay writing?**
    a. Proofreading
    b. Editing
    c. Revising
    d. All of the above

2. **What is the first step to cleaning up your essay?**
    a. Editing
    b. Proofreading
    c. Revising
    d. Submitting

3. **When revising your essay, what do you focus on most?**
    a. The individual sentences
    b. The individual paragraphs
    c. Spelling mistakes
    d. The essay as a whole

4. **What are the two steps of revising?**
    a. Explain
    b. Analyze
    c. Make changes
    d. Both B and C

5. **What does editing focus on?**
    a. How you present your ideas
    b. Style and consistency
    c. Removing spelling and punctuation errors
    d. Both a and b

Chapter 5 Comprehension Quiz

Instructions: Circle the best answer.

6. **What are the two main opponents of concise writing?**
   a. Wordy sentences and bad punctuation
   b. Repetition and wordy sentences
   c. Alliteration and hyperboles
   d. None of the above

7. **What would you NOT do when editing your essay?**
   a. Shorten wordy sentences.
   b. Cut out unnecessary words.
   c. Focus on style and consistency.
   d. Think about the ideas of your essay as a whole.

8. **When proofreading your essay, what do you focus on?**
   a. Your essay ideas as a whole
   b. Small errors, such as spelling mistakes
   c. The way you present your ideas
   d. Whether your essay has flow

9. **What do you need to check when proofreading?**
   a. Spelling errors
   b. Punctuation errors
   c. Grammatical mistakes
   d. All of the above

10. **What is NOT recommended when proofreading your essay?**
    a. Relying on a spell check software
    b. Reading your essay backward
    c. Giving your essay to a family member or friend
    d. Reading the sentences out loud

STEP 5

Going Above and Beyond

STEP 5

CHAPTER 6

Types of Five-Paragraph Essays to Master

Finally, you have completed your five-paragraph essay. Congratulations! At this point, you've researched, outlined, drafted, and cleaned up your essay, so you can finally turn it in to your teacher or hit "submit" on the computer. What a relief!

You may be wondering why there is still more to this book if you've finished writing, right? Well, just because you have completed writing your five-paragraph essay doesn't mean your writing journey has come to an end. There's still much to learn, more than we can cover in this book.

Our goal is to help you become a better writer and equip you with knowledge that will help you excel. That's why this chapter is part of Step 5: Going Above and Beyond.

Remember in Chapter 1 we discussed how Chapters 2-5 were dedicated to providing you with an organizational *blueprint* of the basic five-paragraph essay? Do you remember how we went on to explain this preparatory blueprint carefully lays out a solid structure and framework that can serve as the *basis* for many, specific types of essays?

Well, this is where we are going to put that concept into practice, since you are now well-versed in the basic five-paragraph essay blueprint!

In this chapter, we are going to go above and beyond by investigating four, specific types of essays. We will define each type of essay and explore what makes each one unique. Furthermore, we will use the basic five-paragraph essay blueprint you learned and apply it to the different essay types and model whole-essay examples. That way, you can clearly see how the five-paragraph essay blueprint can be easily adapted and used for different types of essays (Zile, 2006).

An essay is a form of prose writing that develops an idea or argument. Essays can be subdivided into four main categories or subgroups:

6.1.   Expository Essay–Stick to The Facts
6.2.   Narrative Essay–Story Time
6.3.   Descriptive Essay–A Vivid Portrayal
6.4.   Persuasive Essay–Change My Mind

Knowing the type of essay you need to write will keep your essay focused, as each serves a different purpose and requires different styles of writing and criteria. However, they will all keep to the same basic five-paragraph essay structure. We will delve deep and closely examine what differentiates each essay type in the following lessons. Let's get into it!

Lesson 6.1: Expository Essay—Stick to the Facts

The main purpose of an expository essay is to *expose* facts and information. In other words, expository essays require you to present an idea in logical order, making it easy for the reader to understand (Traffis, n.d.).

To write a killer expository essay, you need two skills:

1. The ability to convey information in an easy-to-understand manner
2. In-depth knowledge of the essay topic

This type of essay analyzes a topic utilizing facts only. Therefore, it should be written objectively, without using "I" and "we" or personal opinions and experiences. Typically, first person point of view is not used in expository essay writing. In many cases, however, statistics and scientific studies are referenced in this type of writing.

What are the distinguishing traits of an expository essay?

- **Logical order** that makes sense to the reader (Purdue Writing Lab, n.d.-c)
- **Objective writing** that is backed up by relevant evidence
- **Formal writing** that conveys information without the use of first person point of view
- **Clear explanation** that is easy for the reader to follow

 Study Skill: A true expository essay does not contain contractions. Contractions are utilized more in informal writing.

Expository essays typically follow the same structure as our basic five-paragraph essay blueprint with an introduction that establishes a topic and background information, body paragraphs that present an analysis and factual information, and a conclusion that summarizes key points from the essay (WriteMyEssay4Me.org, 2021).

199

Expository Essay Example

Prompt: Explain the health effects of a plant-based diet.

Title: From Long-Term Disease to a Longer Life: How a Plant-Based Diet Combats Chronic Illnesses

◆━━━━━━━━━━━━━━━━━━━━━━━◆

In the Netflix documentary What The Health, Dr. Michelle McMacken states "...when you look at chronic disease risk, and all of the things that we walk around worrying about—actually dietary choices trump smoking when it comes to those risks" (Friedman, 2017). The typical American diet, which contains a lot of processed, fried, and high-fat animal-based foods, is a major cause of chronic illnesses, many of which are the leading cause of death in the United States (CDC, 2021a; Yang et al., 2015). There is a question, then, for how the American diet can be improved to lower the rate of these illnesses. The key to improving health in the United States is in the connection between diet and disease. A plant-based diet, one that discourages the consumption of animal products and encourages the consumption of fruits, vegetables, and legumes, can help to prevent chronic illnesses, such as obesity, diabetes, and heart disease.

> The introduction kicks off with an interesting quote that directly relates to the essay topic. This grabs the reader's attention immediately.

> The introduction ends with a thesis statement that directly relates to the prompt and presents our three main ideas.

Obesity has become a worldwide epidemic, as the amount of people who are overweight is constantly increasing; however, a plant-based diet can decrease the risk of unhealthy weight gain. An individual with obesity has a Body Mass Index (BMI) of 30.0 kg/m2, while an overweight individual has a BMI of 25.0-29.9 kg/m2. In a trial that introduced a plant-based diet to a community of obese individuals, there was an average BMI decrease of 4.4 kg/m2 over a 6-month period as well as an improvement in cholesterol levels and blood pressure (Wright et al., 2017). There is clear evidence that a plant-based diet can help decrease unhealthy weight. Consequently, this way of eating can help reduce the risk of obesity.

> The topic sentence relates back to one of our three main ideas in the thesis statement (obesity).

> The concluding sentence summarizes the paragraph and links back to the thesis statement.

In addition to reducing the risk of obesity and aiding in weight loss, a plant-based diet has proven to manage and prevent diabetes. In the documentary Forks Over Knives, Dr. Neal Barnard explains the cause of diabetes is not related to consuming too many carbs or too much sugar (Friedman, 2017). Rather, fat buildup in the blood causes diabetes. While a meat-based diet is full of unhealthy fats, a vegan diet is typically low-fat. Dr. Barnard provided evidence for this diet-disease connection in 2006 when he led a trial comparing an American Diabetes Association (ADA) diet with a low-fat vegan diet. Only 26% of people on the ADA diet could reduce diabetes medication usage, while 43% of those on the low-fat vegan diet could do the same (Tuso et al., 2013). This difference is significant, and it shows there may be a better solution to a chronic issue. With that being said, it is clear a plant-based diet is effective in reducing the risk of diabetes.

A plant-based diet high in fiber and antioxidants may also help reduce cardiovascular diseases. Heart disease kills every 1 in 4 people, and its presence in the United States is mostly due to the Western diet, which is high in saturated fats, salt, and cholesterol (Lozano, 2012). However, a ~12-year study showed a plant-based diet can lower the risk of developing serious heart conditions by 32% (Crowe et al., 2013). As people consume more plant-based foods and less animal-based foods, the chances of dying from cardiovascular disease will likely drop below 25%. But, preventing a main cause of death is not the only benefit of a plant-based diet. By eating more high-fiber, high-antioxidant foods, people can see major improvements in their cardiovascular health, no matter their previous risk. Clearly, a plant-based diet has its place in the prevention and reversing of heart disease.

The topic sentence facilitates a smooth transition between body paragraph 1 and body paragraph 2.

Notice the informative language without the use of personal opinion or first person point of view.

The topic sentence is supported by statistics and hard scientific evidence brought in from a reliable study. Notice the citations.

The topic sentence relates back to the third point in the thesis statement (heart disease).

Much scientific evidence suggests a plant-based diet can reduce and even reverse chronic illnesses in the United States, such as obesity, diabetes, and heart disease. Eating more fruits, vegetables, and legumes, while eating fewer animal products, can lead to healthy weight loss, reduce the risk of obesity, prevent and reverse diabetes, and even improve heart health. So, for the general population to heal, it may be better to stop "living to eat" and start "eating to live"(Tuse et al., 2013). The future of health is not in the next pill, injection, or medical procedure, but instead in what lands on people's plates and into their mouths. Only then will there be lasting progress in the prevention of chronic disease.

Lesson 6.1 Exercise: True or False

Instructions: Read the statements about expository essays and decide whether they're true or false.

1. The role of an expository essay is to persuade the reader to change their attitude or behavior about a topic.
a) True
b) False

2. The role of an expository essay is to discuss facts.
a) True
b) False

3. You need two skills to write a great expository essay: ability to convey easily understood information and an in-depth knowledge of the essay topic.
a) True
b) False

4. Expository essays should be written in first person point of view using "I" and "we."
a) True
b) False

5. Expository essays have a plot line and characters.
a) True
b) False

6. One of the distinguishing traits of an expository essay is using a variety of figurative language and techniques.
a) True
b) False

7. Expository essays often utilize statistics and scientific studies.
a) True
b) False

8. It is important to use vivid adjectives and imagery in expository essay writing.
a) True
b) False

Lesson 6.1 Exercise: Write Your Own Essay

Instructions: Write an expository essay for the prompt below.

Prompt: What are the negative effects of social media?

_____

_____

_____

_____

_____

_____

_____

_____

_____

_____

_____

_____

_____

_____

_____

_____

_____

_____

_____

_____

_____

_____

Lesson 6.1 Exercise: Write Your Own Essay

Instructions: Write an expository essay for the prompt below.

Prompt: What are the negative effects of social media?

_____

_____

_____

_____

_____

_____

_____

_____

_____

_____

_____

_____

_____

_____

_____

_____

_____

_____

_____

_____

_____

Lesson 6.2: Narrative Essay—Story Time

A narrative essay is another common essay type you'll likely stumble upon.

This type of essay is typically a personal essay that serves to tell a story of significance to you, the writer. It should be based on events in your life that have impacted you and not be made-up or imaginary. It gives you the opportunity to show your creativity and express your emotions through writing. However, keep in mind you don't write this story aimlessly. It usually includes a moral or bigger-picture lesson the reader can learn from (WriteMyEssay4Me.org, 2021).

Narrative writing tests your skill at writing a story in a clear, cohesive way. Your audience wants a story with a beginning, middle, and end.

When writing your narrative essay, think about the **characters** you want to include, the setting, your **voice**, and whether you want to include a **conflict** (Fleming, 2019b). A conflict helps keep readers enticed and on the edge of their seats. It could be a disagreement between characters, or it could be an internal struggle. This part is not necessary—just something to consider.

What are the distinguishing traits of a narrative essay?

- **A personal touch** that strays from an expository essay by giving you a chance to write in the first person point of view
- **A story** that should be portrayed chronologically for clarity
- **A moral** or underlying lesson the reader can learn from
- **Characters** who each play a role, small or large, in progressing the story
- **A setting** where the narrative or story occurs
- **An expressive tone** that makes for effective storytelling (WriteMyEssay4Me.org, 2021)

Our essay example combines some of these features with the five-paragraph essay blueprint to curate a clear narrative essay. Go ahead and take a look!

Narrative Essay Example

Prompt: What is your favorite cooking memory, and what did you learn from it?

Title: The Power of Cooking: The Story of a Revived Family Tradition

---

All you could hear in the dining room that Friday night was obnoxious laughter. My parents, sisters, brother, and I were as happy as we'd been all day. Let me tell you why. It had been years since my dad cooked one of his signature Persian dishes, and we were all afraid he may never make one again. When he came to the U.S. from Israel to start a family with my mom, he brought endless memories of cooking with my grandmother and an impressive list of recipes. For years, our kitchen smelled like ghormeh sabzi, gondi, and aush reshteh, but my family started eating less meat, and my dad stopped making his dishes. This Friday night, however, we got creative and worked together to create a vegetarian version of ghormeh sabzi, one of his favorite stews. That momentous night, I learned how cooking keeps memories alive, connects you to family, and leads to truly joyful experiences.

> The necessary details to set the story up and provide a background for the claim are presented. The characters are introduced to provide context for the story.

> There is a clear three-point thesis statement, which follows the basic five-paragraph essay blueprint.

Cooking has a funny way of keeping memories alive and fresh. Earlier that day, my siblings and I were doubtful my dad would be motivated to cook again, but when we asked him to help us make the stew, he jumped up with a smile and asked what ingredients we needed. Even though my dad hadn't cooked a Persian dish in years, he returned to his roots and helped us cook. As he stirred the stew with his favorite wooden spoon, I remembered the many times my siblings and I would wait at the table for our parents to place a heaping pot of warm stew in front of us. And I wondered if my dad could remember all the times in Iran and Israel when he crowded around the table with his own siblings and enjoyed what he had made. I hoped making one of his signature dishes helped keep his memories alive like it did mine.

> The topic sentence directly relates to the first point in the thesis statement.

> Narrative essays, despite not being called 'descriptive', should still have some details that allow the reader to visualize what is going on in the story, as in this paragraph.

Not only did I learn how cooking keeps memories alive, but I also learned how it connects you to family. Because my dad grew up cooking with his family, I decided to call his siblings in Israel. I faced the phone camera toward my dad, who was still stirring the stew, and his siblings yelled his name through the phone. He turned around and screamed their names back in sheer delight, and while my sisters and I watched the pot, he told his siblings what we were making. He returned to the kitchen an hour later, and I could tell he was glad I called. Cooking helped him connect with his family in Israel, and it was helping him connect more with us at home. I felt closer to my dad than ever. When he saw the dish was almost done, he said he would handle it from here. It was fine by me! I was just happy to feel so connected to my family.

This paragraph corresponds with the second idea in the thesis statement. This paragraph continues the chronological order of the essay.

Feeling close to my family was great, but I also felt we created a memorable and joyful experience by cooking together. When the stew was done, my mom and my brother grabbed the pot to bring it to the table. In a split second, however, the stew went from the pot to the ground, and all we could hear was the splash of its soupy contents falling onto the floor and under the stove. Everyone looked into each other's eyes with disbelief. Suddenly, we all started laughing uncontrollably! This dish had taken hours of labor, but all it led to was the smell of carpet soaked in ghormeh sabzi. It was hilarious! I fell to the floor laughing, realizing this was a beautiful moment of pure, utter joy with my family. Our day of cooking was the most fun we'd had together all year, and we were not going to let one mistake bring us all down.

The topic sentence links back to the third point in the thesis statement.

Notice the use of evocative language in this paragraph to make the story relatable to the reader.

It's hard for me to think of anything more important than memories, family, and creating fun experiences together, and it is just as difficult to think of anything that can combine those three aspects of life better than cooking does. Memories can get lost, families can grow distant, and joyous experiences can become rare, but they don't have to. That Friday night, I learned how powerful cooking can be and how it can bring people closer together, bring back memories, and create new experiences. I hope my mom, my dad, my sisters, my brother, and I all remember that special Friday night for the rest of our lives.

The conclusion kicks off with a modified, rephrased thesis statement. The closing statement shows the importance of the essay. The writer shows us what this story means to them.

Lesson 6.2 Exercise: Fill in the Blanks

Instructions: Fill in the blanks using the words in the provided word bank.

creativity	personal	personal details
first	lesson	voice
chronological		characters

1. A narrative essay is a _____ essay. It is not fictional.

2. _____, a distinguishing trait of a narrative essay, help to move the story along.

3. Your audience won't understand where you're coming from if you don't use your _____.

4. A great narrative essay should provide your viewpoint in _____ person point of view.

5. The conclusion reminds your reader of the story's _____.

6. In a narrative essay, your body paragraphs should be organized in _____ order.

7. Narrative writing gives you the opportunity to show your _____

8. After your introductory hook, you should bring in _____ that relate to your prompt.

Lesson 6.2 Exercise: Write Your Own Essay

Instructions: Write a narrative essay for the prompt below.

Prompt: Discuss a time when someone treated you unfairly.

Lesson 6.2 Exercise: Write Your Own Essay

Instructions: Write a narrative essay for the prompt below.

Prompt: Discuss a time when someone treated you unfairly.

Lesson 6.3: Descriptive Essay—A Vivid Portrayal

Consider what comes to mind when thinking of a descriptive essay. A detailed description? Imagery? Vivid words? Well, these are all correct.

A descriptive essay paints an intricate picture with *words*. Its purpose is to create an evocative portrayal of a place, object, situation, person, character, or event that engages the reader's senses and stimulates the mind. The reader should be able to visualize the subject or main idea of the essay with ease. Descriptive writing is often an outlet for creativity and imagination, where artistic freedom can run wild with words.

The most effective descriptive essays elicit emotion and strong feelings from the reader. Take note you should use a wide range of vocabulary, so your language is creative, colorful, and original. Oftentimes, this type of essay uses informal language and first person point of view (WriteMyEssay4Me.org, 2021).

Study Skill: Practice descriptive writing by journaling daily. Use vivid adjectives, figurative language techniques, and descriptors to accurately portray your feelings and the day's events.

What are the distinguishing traits of a descriptive essay?

- **Rich detail** that paints a clear picture in the reader's mind with the use of colorful language and descriptive adjectives
- **Figurative language techniques** such as, similes, metaphors, analogies, oxymora, personifications, and onomatopoeia, that are common in creative writing
- **Emotional appeal** that draws the reader in and elicits a powerful, emotionally-charged response
- **Sensory details** that appeal to the five senses of touch, taste, smell, sight, and sound (WriteMyEssay4Me.org, 2021)

Descriptive essays do not have to follow a prescribed structure, but they almost always include important elements, such as an introduction that sets the tone, a descriptive body, and a recap that provides a deeper meaning or insight (WriteMyEssay4Me.org, 2021). However, in our example, we will show you how the basic five-paragraph essay blueprint can be adapted and used to formulate a powerful descriptive essay. Let's get to it!

Descriptive Essay Example

Prompt: Describe a meal that is special to you.

Title: My Take on Traditional Indian Cuisine: The Incredible Spread of Three

Cooking is an exhilarating process that brings flavors together in a perfect symphony. It is an art form that allows you to discover new flavor combinations dancing around your tongue in flawless rhythm. And it is the epitome of family-life in the heart of a home. I grew up in an Indian household where the kitchen air was always filled with the vibrant scent of aromatic curries and bold spices, and my mother was the wizard behind the magic. She could take anything, even the most unorthodox ingredients, and magically make them taste good. Watching her create elaborate dishes laced with love inspired my appreciation for cooking authentic Indian cuisine. There's no doubt her classic spread of tender vegetable biryani, creamy raita chutney, and tangy mirchi ka salan is my absolute favorite.

My mother's vegetable biryani creates the perfect balance of flavors in your mouth. It is a rice dish layered with complex flavors from marinated vegetables, delicate long-grain basmati rice, crispy deep-fried onions, and fragrant spices. Imagine a vibrant medley of carrots, peas, cauliflower, corn, green beans, and potatoes engulfed in a sumptuous bath of yogurt spiced with coriander, cumin, mace, cloves, and turmeric. The vegetables are tenderized from the acid in the yogurt, while the rice is steamed in a pool of perfumed water. Each grain is cooked until soft but not mushy. Then the vegetables and rice are layered together in a pot, with a generous scoop of crunchy onion and freshly chopped mint in between each layer. The mixture is covered with a dome made of dough to be baked in the oven or gently cooked over a low flame, an ancient cooking technique called dum. The process is long and relentless but worth it. It results in a decadent, well-balanced bite in your mouth that is reminiscent of fireworks on the Fourth of July.

The introduction provides background and sets the stage for the rest of the essay. Personal and possessive pronouns like "I" and "my" are used because this is informal writing.

There is a clear three-point thesis statement about the author's favorite foods.

Body paragraph 1 describes the first point in the thesis statement, vegetable biryani. Imagery and vivid language such as "sumptuous," "crunchy," and "perfumed" are used to get the reader engaged and provide rich detail.

214

Now comes the perfect companion to the flavorsome biryani: a cooling raita chutney! To accompany the heat on your tongue from the biryani, my mother's raita offers a sweet and salty taste. A beloved side dish that holds a godly status in every Indian household, it is a brilliant concoction made of velvety dahi (salted yogurt), refreshing herbs, crunchy vegetables, and the intense flavor of crushed garlic and ginger. My mother's recipe calls for the clever addition of pomegranate seeds, which creates a bright pink tone resembling the color of strawberry Nesquik milk. With each silky bite, the pomegranate delivers a punch of tartness and a nutty sweetness. Just like when a fire truck puts out a fiery disaster with water, the ice-cold, creamy raita calms a raging tongue that's been exposed to peppery spices. My mom and I always look forward to the chutney; without it, the spread would be incomplete.

Last but not least is the feisty mirchi ka salan, a special curry my mom makes from roasted nuts and tart water carefully extracted from tamarind. This is the last item in the delectable spread making for the ultimate Indian feast! While vegetable biryani and raita chutney give body to the meal, mirchi ka salan serves as the tangy sidekick. Originating from Hyderabad, India, mirchi ka salan is commonly served with biryani to cut the richness of the rice and provide a contrasting flavor. It's an intensely flavored dish made from the gooey paste of softly toasted coconut, sesame seeds, peanuts, almonds, and dry, red chilies that is slowly simmered with water, tamarind, and long, green chilies until the perfect consistency is reached! Rich in a deep, brown color, full of irresistible flavor, and packed with a punch, this dish will win anyone over. It holds its own in this wonderful spread of three!

The topic sentence seamlessly transitions from Body Paragraph 1 to Body Paragraph 2.

The second to last sentence exhibits the use of figurative language, a simile, when comparing a fire truck's abilities to raita's cooling abilities.

The writer uses tons of adjectives and descriptive words, so the reader can imagine exactly what is being portrayed.

The topic sentence links back to the third point in the thesis statement.

Out of all the classic Indian dishes I have ever had, there has always been something special about my mom's vegetable biryani, raita chutney, and mirchi ka salan that, together, outshine other classics, like chicken tikka masala or aloo gobi. There's no denying the bountiful flavor of vegetable biryani, the cooling satisfaction of raita, or the tangy punch of mirchi ka salan. However, what makes them truly special to me is not their taste, their smell, or their appearance; it's the fact that my mother cooked me these dishes for many years while growing up. Without her, my love for food and Indian cuisine would never have blossomed. This delectable trio shines bright just like my mother, and it will always hold a special place in my heart.

The conclusion starts by rephrasing the thesis statement. It then provides a brief overview of what has been included in the essay. It ends with emotional appeal and an explanation as to why the spread of three is special to the writer. Furthermore, it ties back to the writer's mother, who was mentioned in the introduction.

Lesson 6.3 Exercise: The Five Senses

Instructions: You're given ten different words or phrases. Use adjectives to describe them, thinking about one of the five senses. The first one has been done for you.

Word or Phrase	Sense	Description
Seaside	Smell	Sweet, fresh, crisp, fishy, salty
Flamingo	Sight	
Pizza	Taste	
Sleepover	Hearing	
Bed	Touch	
Castle	Sight	
Garbage	Smell	
Glass of water	Taste	
Hugging	Touch	
An audience clapping	Hearing	
Cat	Touch	

Lesson 6.3 Exercise: Write Your Own Essay

Instructions: Write a descriptive essay for the prompt below.

Prompt: Describe your favorite dessert.

_____

_____

_____

_____

_____

_____

_____

_____

_____

_____

_____

_____

_____

_____

_____

_____

_____

_____

_____

Lesson 6.3 Exercise: Write Your Own Essay

Instructions: Write a descriptive essay for the prompt below.

Prompt: Describe your favorite dessert.

Lesson 6.4: Persuasive Essay—Change My Mind

The purpose of a persuasive essay is to convince the reader to hold the same opinion or point of view about something as you do. It may be persuading your reader to think in a certain way or to follow a direction and act.

In a persuasive essay, although you can express your personal opinions, you must support and validate these opinions with evidence. Otherwise, your reader will have no reason to believe what you say. Evidence can be facts, examples, or depictions.

Persuasive writing is often used in editorial pieces, like BuzzFeed articles, and advertising. In many cases, this type of writing can be more casual and informal, especially compared to expository writing. You want your reader to feel like they can relate to you as the writer, so powerful, evocative language is important as well (Traffis, n.d.).

Furthermore, it is necessary to present your opinion as the *only* plausible one to convince your reader! Persuasive writing is subjective by nature. It will not hold an objective tone, like expository writing.

What are the distinguishing traits of a persuasive essay?

- **A crystal-clear viewpoint** that is the only plausible argument, so the reader doesn't have to guess or be bombarded with other viewpoints
- **Relevant, reliable pieces of information** that support your point of view, whether facts, examples, or depictions
- **Emotionally charged language** that is powerful and will help persuade the reader (MasterClass Staff, 2022)
- **Casual tone** that can be less formal than expository writing

Persuasive Essay Example

Prompt: Should teens learn how to cook before they move out?

Title: Why a Teenager like You Needs to Learn How to Cook Now

◆ - ◆

Cooking isn't always glamorous. It's usually something you have to do so you can get to the good part: eating. Oftentimes, it can be a chore that requires washing endless pots and pans. And other times, it's frustrating because you actually have to do the action of cooking instead of turning toward the convenience of frozen pizzas and ordering takeout. When you finally get to adulthood and live on your own, though, it's too late. You don't know how to cook or where to begin. That's why it's imperative for you, as a teenager, to learn how to cook while you're still in adolescence. By learning how to cook before you are on your own, you can improve your budgeting skills, become more independent, and develop a habit of mindful eating.

> Notice how the introduction speaks directly to the audience and uses language the audience understands to lead them into the essay. Then, the argument is presented.

> There are three clear points in the thesis statement.

> The topic sentence addresses the first point in the thesis statement.

You should learn how to cook before you are on your own because your budgeting skills will improve while you can still afford to make mistakes. A meal cannot be prepared without the necessary ingredients, and you can learn to become financially adept when grocery shopping for these ingredients. A benefit of eating at home rather than eating out is that it is generally cheaper, but a trip to the grocery store can be more expensive if you are buying large amounts of perishable items that may go to waste or buying items you may not actually need. By cooking for yourself and learning grocery tips and tricks—such as buying smaller quantities of perishable items or buying in-season produce—you will have a solid budgeting plan for when you are more financially independent. Clearly, cooking is more than what happens in the kitchen, and it provides adolescents like you with a taste of financial responsibility.

> Notice how this paragraph brings up a concern the reader may have, and then shows how the main argument of the essay addresses that concern (i.e., expensive grocery trips). This helps persuade the reader.

Cooking can also teach you to be more independent while you still have a cushion of dependence at home. It is easy to get into a routine of always relying on parents or older siblings to make food, but family members won't always be around when hunger kicks in. Taking some initiative to learn how to cook will help you rely more on yourself and be more independent. You may be concerned your cooking skills are not up to par, but preparing food can improve self-esteem (Carnegie Mellon University, n.d.). For example, when you cook lunch daily, you will learn how to make delicious recipes and may even experiment with flavors as you get more comfortable. This will make you more confident in your ability to cook well, and it will teach you to be more self-sufficient. It's a win-win situation.

> The topic sentence links back to the second point in the thesis statement.

> This paragraph brings in evidence to support the topic sentence, and the paragraph ends with a reminder of the main argument.

Equally important, cooking also helps you develop a habit of mindful eating. Ultimately, you decide what you put in your body. However, if you have never cooked for yourself, then you have never had complete control over what you eat. It's likely you eat whatever your school or parents have prepared for you, but when you cook for yourself, you will become more aware of what ingredients go into your food and what you're putting into your body. Through mindful eating, you will become more intentional about buying healthy food, cooking healthy food, and eating healthy food. If you want to be a mindful eater—to be in control of what you eat—then you have to be involved in the whole process.

> The topic sentence seamlessly transitions from Body Paragraph 2 to Body Paragraph 3.

> This is a good use of powerful language that may make the reader more emotionally invested in the argument.

Living at home, with no immediate incentive to start budgeting, gain more independence, or eat mindfully, it may seem like there is all the time in the world before you should start taking more responsibility and learn how to cook. You should avoid this fantasy! It is imperative you learn to cook for yourself while still in adolescence to prepare yourself for real life. If you don't learn this essential skill, the stakes will only get higher as you find yourself unprepared for adulthood. Cooking will teach you to budget properly, feel confident and independent, and eat mindfully and healthily while you are still young. You can try to avoid touching a pan or a wooden spoon until you're older, or you can embrace cooking with open arms and start to see its powerful impact on your life.

Chapter 6 Takeaway: Now that you have seen how one common theme, like food, can be utilized to write four distinct essays, you should have a clear understanding of how the four types of essays we covered in Chapter 6 (expository, narrative, descriptive, and persuasive) are different from one another. You should also have a better grasp of how the basic five-paragraph essay blueprint can be loosely followed to help structure and organize different types of essays.

Lesson 6.4 Exercise: True or False

Instructions: Read the statements about persuasive essays and decide whether they're true or false.

1. The purpose of a persuasive essay is to convince the reader to hold the same opinion as you about the essay topic.
a) True
b) False

2. Persuasive essays and expository essays have the same tone.
a) True
b) False

3. Your persuasive essay will be convincing even if the argument is unclear.
a) True
b) False

4. In persuasive essay writing, you need to evoke emotions in the reader instead of simply stating facts.
a) True
b) False

5. Every piece of evidence in a persuasive essay must be based on scholarly research.
a) True
b) False

6. Persuasive essay writing is objective.
a) True
b) False

7. Persuasive writing is often used in editorial pieces and advertising.
a) True
b) False

8. In a persuasive essay, you must support and validate your opinions with evidence.
a) True
b) False

Lesson 6.4 Exercise: Write Your Own Essay

Instructions: Write a persuasive essay for the prompt below.

Prompt: Should children get paid for doing household chores?

Lesson 6.4 Exercise: Write Your Own Essay

Instructions: Write a persuasive essay for the prompt below.

Prompt: Should children get paid for doing household chores?

_____

_____

_____

_____

_____

_____

_____

_____

_____

_____

_____

_____

_____

_____

_____

_____

_____

_____

_____

_____

_____

_____

Chapter 6 Comprehension Quiz

Instructions: Circle the best answer.

1. **How many main essay types are there?**
    a. Two
    b. Nine
    c. Four
    d. Five

2. **What is the main aim of an expository essay?**
    a. To persuade the reader
    b. To tell a story
    c. To expose facts and information
    d. To give a description of an event

3. **Do you write in first or third person point of view in an expository essay?**
    a. Both
    b. Third person point of view
    c. Neither
    d. First person point of view

4. **What is a narrative essay most similar to?**
    a. Telling a story with a moral
    b. Writing a formal report
    c. A call to action
    d. An argument

5. **What are important factor(s) to consider when writing a narrative essay?**
    a. A moral
    b. Characters
    c. Your voice
    d. All of the above

6. **What is the role of a descriptive essay?**
   a. To persuade the reader
   b. To make an argument
   c. To tell a story
   d. To provide a detailed description of a place, object, situation, person, character, or event

7. **What should you include in a descriptive essay to create vivid imagery?**
   a. Long, drawn-out sentences
   b. Figurative language
   c. Statistics
   d. Scientific evidence

8. **What is the role of a persuasive essay?**
   a. To tell a story
   b. To describe an event or person to the reader
   c. To expose facts
   d. To convince the reader

9. **What is a trait of persuasive essays?**
   a. Emotionally charged language
   b. A setting
   c. Sensory details
   d. Characters

10. **Which essay type uses imagery and vivid adjectives?**
    a. Persuasive essay
    b. Expository essay
    c. Descriptive Essay
    d. Narrative Essay

CHAPTER 7

Going Pro with Essay Writing

Now that your essay is complete, and you've learned the different types of essays, you're going to learn some cool techniques and tips on how to write the best essay you possibly can. As this chapter is purely informational, it won't be interactive like the previous chapters and will not have end-of-lesson exercises. This is part of Step 5: Going Above and Beyond.

At this point, your essay is complete, and you can submit it if you haven't already. However, this chapter is here to give you some extra knowledge and an *edge* to your writing. It builds on everything you have learned thus far.

This chapter covers the following:

7.1.	Making Your Writing More Creative
7.2.	Adding Your Voice
7.3.	Reflecting on What You've Done
7.4.	Reading the "Write" Way

Let's get started!

Lesson 7.1: Making Your Writing More Creative

Most essays ask you to present facts and be objective. However, that doesn't mean you can't be creative with your writing! We'll go over some tips you can use to add that punch of creativity to your writing.

Tips on Adding Creativity

Follow these three general tips to add creativity to your academic writing:

1. **Introduce new vocabulary using a thesaurus.**

A thesaurus is great if your essay is struggling with repetition or you're not able to recall the exact word you're after. Using words from a thesaurus can make your essay sound more sophisticated, but make sure you know what each word means!

2. **Bring in personal experience (if appropriate).**

Bringing in personal experience may enrich your argument for some academic essays. But, the important word here is SOME! If you've been told to write a formal essay on a serious topic, the likelihood is you'll need to remain objective and not mention yourself.

3. **Use imagery.**

The goal of imagery is to paint a clear picture in the reader's mind, to make them feel like they are immersed in your writing. Descriptive words, like adjectives, can pull your reader in and help them imagine the picture you're trying to create.

Similes and metaphors are great creative techniques to use as well. But this depends on the type of essay you're writing. Similes and metaphors are great in descriptive essays, but they typically don't belong in expository essays.

A simile compares two things using "as" or "like." For example, "his smile was like the sunshine" or "light as a feather."

A metaphor is when you describe something as if it *is* something else. Here are a couple of examples: "He is sunshine," or "It was an emotional rollercoaster."

Now, let's look at two versions of a paragraph that utilize imagery. After you've read them, decide which one you enjoyed and which one doesn't really capture your attention.

Example 1: Thanksgiving at my house is great! I help my mom in the morning, throw decorations around to make things look pretty, set the table, and put on good clothes. After a long time, I finally sit down at the table with my family, and we give thanks and eat. We eat turkey, mashed potatoes, and even pie too! The best part is spending time with my family and feeling happy together. Every year, Thanksgiving gets better. Maybe you'll want to join next time.

Example 2: The aroma of hot, ready-to-serve turkey, creamy garlic mashed potatoes, and sweet, crunchy pecan pie fills your nose. It makes your taste buds jump and fills you with a comforting warmth that only comes with good ol' home cooking and family. That's what Thanksgiving is like in my home. I start the morning dancing around the kitchen, helping my mom crack eggs for the magnificent feast in the evening. *Whoosh*– then I zip through the house, putting up decor and setting the table with the finest china we own. I put on my best clothes and make sure to wear the emerald-green necklace my dad gave me as a special gift. I count the hours until I can sit down at the table with my family, each passing hour more agonizing than the one before. Finally, after what seems like a lifetime, I see my beautiful family gathered around the table by the golden fireplace and join them. Together, we give thanks for the blessings in our lives and the meal we get to share. I will never forget the joy and laughter that fills the air. Yet, it seems, every year Thanksgiving only gets better. It's like a warm hug on a cold winter day. I bet you'd like to join, wouldn't you?

So, which one is better? The first one is more concise and does the job of introducing Thanksgiving, but it's not as well-written and enticing as the second version. In the second example, the words jump out at you. You are able to picture a vivid Thanksgiving with delicious food. You are pulled into the writing. There's even a simile describing Thanksgiving like a warm hug! While some imagery is used in the first example, it's not anywhere near the level of the second example.

Final Words of Advice

Definitely make your writing creative...but be careful. Adding too much fluffy language and exaggerations can undermine the main message of your essay. Identify what type of essay your prompt requires and whether creative techniques are appropriate.

Study Skill: When rereading your essay in the revising, editing, and proofreading stages, you'll notice if you've used too many creative writing techniques because they'll stick out like a sore thumb.

Lesson 7.2: Adding Your Voice

Adding your own unique voice to your writing also fits under the creativity umbrella. It has its own lesson because it's easy to get swept up in what *other* writers do when the focus is creativity.

This lesson is all about you. It's about making *your* writing unique by adding *your* individual voice.

If you read any two pieces of writing of the same genre and topic, they'll sound different. This is because different authors have different *voices*.

Having a prominent voice in your writing allows you to stand out from the crowd. It makes your writing interesting and memorable.

But it's not easy finding your voice. Let's go through some steps to help you identify your voice!

Before we do, here's a word of warning: These tips are more relevant to personal essays (i.e., narrative essays) than academic essays. That's why we brought you the basics first in the previous chapters. When you get to the point where you think you can take your writing to the next level, this chapter is here for you!

Step 1: Identify Your Audience

You'll already have done this in Lesson 2.3. Go back over your notes to remind yourself of who your audience is. Knowing your audience will help you make your writing more specific and decide whether you want your voice to be formal or informal.

If you were writing a blog post for animal lovers, you might start it like this:

What's up, fellow animal lovers? Today, we'll be talking about the most popular dog breeds. I have a chocolate lab myself. I know; they're the cutest.

However, you wouldn't even think about writing like that for an academic essay! In an academic essay, you need an **academic voice.** This is an objective and authoritative voice supported with solid evidence.

Academic voice may look like this:

Food consumption in the U.S. population has increased drastically. The average U.S. citizen now weighs around 15 pounds more than they did 20 years ago (Barclay, et al., 2018).

Can you see how the voice here is formal and objective compared to the informal, friendly blog post? It doesn't use "I" or personal opinion but, instead, presents an idea supported by evidence.

Step 2: Strengthen Your Voice

Have you ever read a book where the author has a weak voice? If you're getting bored because you feel the writer is rambling on, it's likely they have a dull voice.

Weak-voiced authors use words that are fluffy and have little meaning. Their main ideas get lost, so they're hard to identify. Here's an example:

It is a good idea to start working at a young age for a number of reasons. The first reason is so you can become more of an independent person.

On the other hand, a strong voice is clear and concise. It communicates the writer's voice well, using precise language.

Writers tend to have a clear voice when they have a finite understanding of the message they want to convey. As you go through this book and write essays, you'll likely develop a strong voice with practice.

Take a look back over the main ideas in your essay. Do you state your ideas clearly in as few words as possible?

Now, let's transform the weak voice example from earlier into a strong voice:

Starting work at a young age increases independence.

We've shortened this down from 30 words to eight. Without the jumble of unnecessary words, the reader can clearly understand what your point is.

Step 3: Reread Your Favorite Books

This sounds like a trick, right? Who wouldn't want to reread their favorite books?

However, you're likely to discover why a particular book is your favorite. When you're rereading it, focus in on the author's voice. What makes their voice unique and one you enjoy?

Here are a couple of things to look out for:

1. Choice of words: Does the author use lots of sensory words? Emotive words? Contrasting words?
2. Imagery: Does the author paint a picture of what they mean using imagery?
3. Perspective: Can you tell the writer's perspective throughout the book? How do they present it?
4. Rhythm: Does the author use long or short sentences or a mixture of both? Does the author use repetition or lots of one-word sentences?

See if you can include some of these techniques in your own writing. But remember, only use these if they're appropriate for your essay type!

Lesson 7.3: Reflecting on What You've Done

As you continue to become a better writer, looking back at your work is important. You may not have any desire to look at your essay again after submitting it, but you will absolutely learn some things about yourself if you do.

You might learn about your writing or thought process, and this can be beneficial for future essays you write.

Effective writing is an important skill no matter where life takes you, so allow yourself to look back at what you've done. Reflect on your struggles, achievements, setbacks, and successes.

Throughout this writing journey, you didn't just become better at turning in an amazing essay. You became a better writer. You got better at overcoming the mental and emotional battles of writing an essay. Be proud of yourself for what you've accomplished.

Reflection gives you more independence. It allows you to critique your own work, rather than relying on feedback from your teacher, parent, peer, or reader. It can also help you identify things you want to tweak slightly.

Here's a reflection table to help you get started.

Reflection Table	
Prompts	**Reflections**
What have I learned from writing this essay?	
What activities did I complete that helped me learn?	
What activities did I find engaging?	
What parts did I really struggle with?	
What was easier than I expected it to be?	
What improvements have I made compared to the last time I wrote an essay?	
What could I do differently next time?	
Does my essay meet the teacher's/ reader's expectations?	

When you're reflecting, remember to **stay positive.** Even if you didn't get everything right this time, your capabilities aren't set in stone. You have plenty of space to grow. Reflection helps you in this growth process.

Lesson 7.4: Reading the "Write" Way

One of the most effortless ways of improving your writing is to read. Making reading a hobby can boost your writing style from good to excellent.

Don't worry. It's normal to be skeptical, as this sounds too good to be true. However, there is a plethora of evidence proving the positive impact reading has on writing. Let's take a look at some.

Voice

As we talked about in Lesson 7.2, reading can help you develop your voice in your writing. We won't go over all the benefits of adding your voice again, but it's important to remember it makes your writing unique and, therefore, memorable.

Vocabulary

When you read, you take in hundreds, if not thousands, of different words. You're exposed to words you wouldn't usually come across.

The context of the book helps you see exactly how the word is used. You can often work out a word's meaning because of its context, even if you've never heard it before. These are called *context clues*.

Constant exposure to new words along with the understanding of their meaning through context improves your mental dictionary and allows you to build a colorful vocabulary (JRE Library, 2017).

Grammar

Just like vocabulary, punctuation and grammar can't be avoided when you read. When you read, you subconsciously digest how authors have used punctuation and grammar in their writing. This improves your understanding of when these important writing elements should be used.

The awareness of punctuation and grammar you've developed will then appear in your writing, as you'll be using these elements effectively to improve the quality and content of your writing (Modern Language Association [MLA] Style Center, 2020).

Critical Thinking

While reading, you can ask yourself whether you think the author is displaying good writing skills. Whatever your answer, be curious about it. Why do you think the writing is good or bad?

Think about your favorite books. What makes them so great? Is it the authors' voices or the creative techniques they've used? Are you really fascinated by the topic?

This will help you in the revising, editing, proofreading, and reflection stages, as you'll be able to think critically about your own work and identify where your writing needs improvement (MasterClass Staff, 2021).

 Study Skill: Reading should still be fun! Don't burden yourself by stopping and taking notes on everything you notice.

Chapter 7 Comprehension Quiz

Instructions: Circle the best answer.

1. **How can you add creativity to your writing?**
   a. Use imagery.
   b. Bring in personal experience when appropriate.
   c. Use a thesaurus.
   d. All of the above

2. **What is a simile?**
   a. When you describe something as if it is something else
   b. When you exaggerate something
   c. When you compare two things using "as" or "like"
   d. A descriptive noun

3. **What is a metaphor?**
   a. When you describe something as if it is something else
   b. When you exaggerate something
   c. When you compare two things using "as" or "like"
   d. A descriptive noun

4. **What are the benefits of a strong voice?**
   a. Makes your writing more unique
   b. Makes your writing more creative
   c. Allows you to voice your strong opinions in an informal way
   d. Both A and B

5. **Why is identifying your audience important when adding your voice?**
   a. You can decide whether you want to write formally or informally.
   b. It allows you to make your writing more specific.
   c. It allows you to generalize your writing.
   d. Both A and B

Chapter 7 Comprehension Quiz

Instructions: Circle the best answer.

6. **Why is reflecting on your work important?**
   a. It makes you feel bad about your mistakes.
   b. It doesn't help you.
   c. It helps you become a better writer.
   d. It's necessary before submitting your work.

7. **What question(s) should you ask yourself when reflecting?**
   a. What have I learned while writing this essay?
   b. What could I do differently next time?
   c. What activities helped me learn?
   d. All of the above

8. **What is NOT a positive effect of reading on writing?**
   a. It helps you identify your voice.
   b. It tells you exactly how you should write your essay.
   c. It improves your grammar and punctuation.
   d. It improves your vocabulary.

9. **How does reading improve your vocabulary?**
   a. It shows you how writers use punctuation.
   b. Continual exposure to new words
   c. You can identify a word's meaning through its context.
   d. Both B and C

10. **Is it always appropriate to apply creative techniques to your writing?**
    a. Yes, creative techniques like similes and metaphors should always be used.
    b. No, creative techniques are not always appropriate.
    c. It is only appropriate if the reader loses interest in your writing.
    d. Creative techniques should only be used in one half of your essay.

Final Thoughts

You've worked through all five overarching steps on how to write a five-paragraph essay! Feel free to scream and cheer because it has taken some grit and hard work! Your brain is now brimming with information sure to make your essays spectacular.

You've planned your essay in detail, brainstorming ideas using brainwriting and webbing. You became an expert in essay research. You've outlined your way to success using traditional methods, and you got creative with different graphic organizers.

You wrote your essay using a careful step-by-step process. First, you uncovered the components of the introduction, including a killer hook to kick off your awesome essay. You developed your thesis statement and learned how to expand this in your body paragraphs by providing evidence for your claims. You analyzed your evidence carefully to lead the reader down the path you wanted them to take, and you achieved a smooth flow using transitions.

In the conclusion, you rephrased, wrapped up your points, and tied them all together like a present with a neat bow.

You came up with a catchy title to draw your reader in and cited and referenced your sources to perfection.

If that weren't enough, you revised, edited, and proofread your work. You improved the fluidity of your essay by cutting out unnecessary words and phrases. You removed punctuation and grammar mistakes until your essay was sparkly clean and mistake free!

You grappled with all the different types of essays—expository, narrative, descriptive, and persuasive. You charmed the reader with creativity, persuasion, and oh so many facts!

And finally, you went "pro" with creative techniques like illustration and exemplification. You added your voice to make your essay unique, and you spent some much needed time reflecting.

And now you're here. You now understand learning to write organized, coherent, and engaging essays is a journey of failures and triumphs, frustrations and rewards, and laughing and crying even!

Keep smiling, knowing thousands of people share the same struggles as you. Becoming a better writer is not a linear path. It requires consistent effort, practice, and belief in your capabilities. You are powerful. Just remember, when you put pen to paper, magic ignites.

We believe in you.

You have this guide forever now. If there are concepts you forget or need to refresh your memory on, just review the section again, and keep pushing forward.

Essential Evaluation Guide for Teachers (and Homeschoolers!)

There's no doubt *you* teachers and homeschoolers already have some resources on how to evaluate essays. But there are more! This chapter provides some handy tips, tricks, and extra guidance that will be beneficial for you along the way.

First, we take you through the eight "must-dos" for evaluating your students' essays. Following these eight essentials will ensure your students flourish (and not flounder) as a result of your feedback.

Then, we explore the ins and outs of rubrics, so you can create one for yourself. You'll be given an example rubric and a blank one to use at your disposal.

So, let's get into it.

EDUCATOR'S LOUNGE

Eight Must-Dos When Evaluating Student Essays

1. Be clear about your expectations.

For a student to understand what they did wrong, they need to know what you expect of them. Here are a few things to consider:

- **Purpose:** Tell your students why they're writing the essay. They need to know why it's important and what they'll learn while writing it.
- **Your goals:** Talk to your students about what your ultimate aim is for this essay. Make the goals relatable to them by exploring how the goals you set add to their learning.
- **How you assess:** Speak to your students about what tools and parameters you'll use to evaluate them. This can help some students understand what's needed or required to be successful.

2. Be encouraging.

Providing feedback isn't easy. It can be taken grudgingly by some students. However, feedback can be framed in a way that is encouraging rather than discouraging.

Yes, you need to give them an adequate depiction of their errors. However, you don't need to point out every individual mistake. You don't want their essay to be littered with a million trivial corrections. Instead, pinpoint the biggest errors, and go from there.

With evaluating essays, think about each student individually. What improvements have they made since their last essay? Did you notice their introduction was attention-grabbing and exciting? Tell them!

Encouraging feedback interspersed between the constructive feedback will make all the difference when they read over the corrections.

Additionally, try to steer clear of percentage or letter grades! Students have a habit of whizzing down to the bottom and only paying attention to that. However, this is difficult to avoid in traditional school settings. The workaround to this is giving meaningful feedback and offering help to your students if they have questions about the corrections or the grade.

3. Put yourself in your student's shoes.

After leaving feedback, take another look over it. Ask yourself, "How would I feel if I was the student reading this?"

Are there enough bouts of genuine encouragement? Or, is the overall feel of the feedback negative? Have you pointed out every single individual flaw or focused primarily on the main errors?

Remember, you want to motivate your students to do better with your feedback. You don't want to destroy all their confidence!

4. Focus on the task at hand.

It's your job to evaluate your students' essays. You're not an editor. So, focus on whether your students met the brief.

Did they succeed in focusing on the prompt set for them? Did they write a relevant thesis statement and relate back to it throughout their essay?

You want to pick up on the fundamental and structural mistakes they made. What parts didn't meet the brief? Issues with spelling and grammar can be focused on at a later time (unless it's an essay for English!). Just tell them how they met the criteria, where they fell short, and what they can do to improve.

Encourage your students to self-evaluate. Show them the revising, editing, and proofreading sections of this book, and inspire them to reflect on their work with Lesson 7.3!

5. Provide specific feedback.

The ultimate goal is for students to meet the requirements of the essay. Keep this in mind all the way through the evaluation. Think about the growth trajectory of each student.

You need to make your feedback specific to each student. What are achievable goals for that particular student? Are you writing comments the student is going to understand?

If you think one comment will be difficult for them to understand, model how you want it to look. For example, if your student has written a hook that's not attention grabbing, write one that *is* and highlight the differences.

6. Critique the writing, not the writer.

When evaluating essays, don't bash the student for all the things they're not particularly good at yet. Saying "you're bad at introductions" doesn't help them grow. It's more likely to knock their confidence.

Instead, focus on their writing. So, rather than telling them they're bad at introductions, you can say, "Your introduction didn't fully meet the essay requirements, but there are ways to improve."

By switching to this style of feedback, you're saying the mistake was made by them but isn't a part of them—it's changeable.

7. Recognize and address common writing issues you're seeing across several students' essays.

Providing feedback for the whole class helps to show students they're not alone. Yes, they made this mistake, but so many others have made it, too!

You could work through the issue as an entire class, not naming any names, but providing the support to multiple students who need it.

This reduces the self-criticism, which is so easy for students to slip into when receiving feedback. It makes it clear to them they're not the only one making mistakes, which makes feedback easier to take in.

8. Create an objective and fair rubric.

We're sure you're very familiar with rubrics. They're the charts used to grade essays and other assignments. Rubrics are handy, as they allow teachers and homeschoolers to grade work with no specific right or wrong answer.

Rubrics typically include the following:

- The expectations of the assignment
- A list of grading criteria
- Varying performance levels

Rubrics make grading easy for you and feedback easy to understand for your students.

There are two main types of rubrics: **holistic** and **analytic**. We recommend analytic rubrics because they help you stay specific. And, just as we mentioned in the fifth must-do, being specific is essential.

A holistic rubric uses one criterion that assesses the student's overall achievement for the assignment set. Students are given a document with paragraphs explaining what is required of them.

An analytic rubric breaks the assignment into chunks. It looks at the different skills vital for the essay and shows your students what's required of them to reach different performance levels.

Analytic rubrics are clearer and easier to understand than holistic rubrics. If your students understand their feedback, they're more likely to improve as a result! Analytic rubrics are also a great visual of your priorities; they help you grade more consistently!

Next, you'll learn how to create your own rubric.

The Rubric

Now that you're clear on what a rubric's purpose is, you can focus on making one yourself.

When creating your own rubric, there are four steps you need to follow:

1. Be clear about the assignment's purpose.
2. Determine the criteria you're going to use to evaluate.
3. Set performance levels.
4. Show your students the rubric.

1. Be clear about the assignment's purpose.

To create a rubric your students will understand, *you* need to understand *why* you're asking them to write this assignment. With this in mind, think about how you can break your expectations down.

Are there some expectations that are more important than others? What do your students need to do to reach different performance levels?

2. Determine the criteria you're going to use to evaluate.

The learning objectives and your expectations of this assignment can be used to build your criteria. Think about the key skills you want your students to demonstrate in the assignment.

Only include the most important factors. A rubric with 50 different criteria won't help anyone! Aim for four to seven criteria. This will show the students the most important factors to focus on and will prevent them from getting bored when attempting to understand their feedback!

Write the criteria in a clear, coherent way, so they're easy to understand. Tailor each learning objective and expectation to the rubric. Can you phrase it in a way which makes it simple for the students to improve?

For example, for an expository essay, your criteria may be as follows:

- Content of introduction
- Content of body paragraphs
- Content of conclusion
- Organization
- Development of ideas
- Quality of writing

3. Set performance levels.

You can't have a rubric without performance levels! Decide on the scale you want to use. You'll typically see three to five performance levels on a rubric.

You could use a combination of numbers and one-word descriptions, or you could use just one of those. You could also use percentages or letter grades—whatever suits your way of grading!

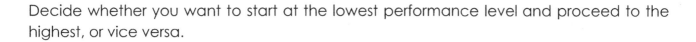

Decide whether you want to start at the lowest performance level and proceed to the highest, or vice versa.

Here's an example:

(1) Does not meet expectations	(2) Meets some expectations	(3) Meets most expectations	(4) Meets/exceeds expectations

4. Show your students the rubric.

Now, when we say show your students the rubric, we mean *before* they write the essay. You need to allow them time to look over the rubric, so they know the following:

- The purpose of the essay
- Your expectations
- What is needed to achieve each performance level

You could go through the rubric with the whole class to make sure they understand what each criterion means.

They can then refer back to the rubric while writing their essays to make sure they're meeting the requirements.

Let's take a look at a completed rubric for you to use as a guide.

	(1) Needs improvement	(2) Proficient	(3) Advanced	(4) Outstanding
Content of Introduction	The introduction lacks at least one key component (i.e. hook, background information, thesis)	The hook, background information, and thesis statement are there, but they are not fully engaging and interesting.	All components of the introduction are present and are engaging to read.	All components are well-thought-out and original. The hook is engaging, the background information is interesting, and the thesis is clear and concise.
Content of Body Paragraphs	Body paragraphs are missing some components and/or do not directly relate to the prompt/thesis statement.	The topic sentence, supporting information, analysis, and concluding sentence are there but lack coherence or are not clear and concise.	All components are present. They are presented in a clear, concise way and relate to the prompt and thesis statement.	All components are present. The reader can clearly see each component, and there is a natural flow between the writer's points.
Content of Conclusion	The conclusion is missing a component (rephrased thesis statement, summary of main points, closing statement) or the writer has included new information.	The thesis statement has been written, but not rephrased. Some of the key points have been mentioned, but not others.	The conclusion includes a rephrased thesis statement, summary of key points, and a concluding sentence.	The conclusion rephrases the thesis statement in an interesting way, and all the key points have been mentioned, showing great understanding from the writer.
Organization	The paragraphs are not in the correct order. Components of the paragraphs have been swapped around, or aspects are missing.	The paragraphs and components are in the right order, but the essay lacks flow.	The paragraphs and components are in the right order, and it is clear the writer has revised, edited, and proofread because the essay has good flow.	Each paragraph flows seamlessly onto the next, with no jumping from one idea to another. Every sentence has a place, with no unnecessary words or phrases.
Development of Ideas	Adequate evidence has not been provided for each of the main ideas.	Each idea has been backed up with some evidence, but this evidence is weak.	Strong evidence has been provided for each idea.	Each idea stated in the thesis statement has been fully explored throughout the essay in an organized and formulaic manner.
Quality of Writing (including transitions)	The quality of the writing is lacking: • Transitions have not been included. • Repeated wrong word choice • Jumpy ideas and general lack of flow • Not written in a clear, concise way	Transitions have been included, and word choice has been good overall, but there are still some errors.	Transitions have been included, and word choice is correct; however, there are still some improvements that could be made to the overall flow and conciseness of the writing.	The whole essay flows well, the writer's words are all relevant, and they have written in a clear, concise manner.

*You don't need to use all the boxes, but they're here if you need them!

253

References

Abraham, M. (2020, October 10). *How anxiety can cause forgetfulness*. CalmClinic. https://www.calmclinic.com/anxiety/symptoms/forgetfulness

Ackerman, C. (2021). *Growth mindset vs. fixed + key takeaways from Dweck's book*. PositivePsychology.com. https://positivepsychology.com/growth-mindset-vs-fixed-mindset/

Ariana, A. (2015). Webbing technique to improve the students' writing recount. *Exposure Journal, 4*(2), 156–179. https://doi.org/10.26618/ejpbi.v4i2.924

Arquilevich, G. (1999). *How to write an essay*. Teacher Created Resources.

Barclay, E., Belluz, J., & Zarracina, J. (2018, August 9). It's easy to become obese in America. These seven charts explain why. *Vox*. https://www.vox.com/2016/8/31/12368246/obesity-america-2018-charts

BBC. (2011, August 24). *Why are earthquakes dangerous?* https://www.bbc.co.uk/newsround/14649717

BBC. (2017, May 15). *Quake: 12 surprising facts about earthquakes*. https://www.bbc.co.uk/programmes/articles/1SILY6lpq5vgxXNXfVIJSvq/12-surprising-facts-about-earthquakes

Behavioral Nutrition. (2020, February 25). *What are carbohydrates and why we need them in our diet*. https://behavioralnutrition.org/healthy-eating-with-carbohydrates/

Bolt, B. (2021, February 1). Earthquake. In *Britannica*. https://www.britannica.com/science/earthquake-geology

Brennan, D. (2020, September 17). *Health benefits of pomegranates*. WebMD. https://www.webmd.com/diet/health-benefits-pomegranates

Britannica. (n.d.). *Know about the concept of the observable universe and on measuring the observable universe within the whole universe* [Video]. https://www.britannica.com/video/185400/universe

Britannica. (2021, September 27). *German-Soviet nonaggression pact*. https://www.britannica.com/event/German-Soviet-Nonaggression-Pact

Carnegie Mellon University. (n.d.). *Cooking as a tool for stimulating development in early childhood education*. Children's School, Department of Psychology, Dietrich College of Humanities and Social Sciences. Retrieved March 25, 2022, from https://www.cmu.edu/dietrich/psychology/cs/program/curriculum/cooking.html

Centers for Disease Control and Prevention. (2020, January 31). *Women and heart disease*. https://www.cdc.gov/heartdisease/women.htm

Centers for Disease Control and Prevention. (2021a, April 28). *About chronic diseases.* https://www.cdc.gov/chronicdisease/about/index.htm

Centers for Disease Control and Prevention. (2021b, October 29). *Health effects of cigarette smoking.* https://www.cdc.gov/tobacco/data_statistics/fact_sheets/health_effects/effects_cig_smoking/index.htm

Chudasama Y. (2011). Animal models of prefrontal-executive function. *Behavioral Neuroscience, 125*(3), 327–343. https://doi.org/10.1037/a0023766

Coppola, D. (2021, October 13). *United States: Number of digital shoppers 2016–2021.* Statista. https://www.statista.com/statistics/183755/number-of-us-internet-shoppers-since-2009/

Crowe, F.L., Appleby, P.N., Travis, R.C., & Key, T.J. (2013, January 30). Risk of hospitalization or death from ischemic heart disease among British vegetarians and nonvegetarians: Results from the EPIC-Oxford cohort study. *The American Journal of Clinical Nutrition, 97*(3), 597–603. https://doi.org/10.3945/ajcn.112.044073

Cunnah, L. (2020a). How to improve memory with mind maps. AYOA. https://www.ayoa.com/ourblog/how-to-improve-memory-with-mind-maps/

Cunnah, L. (2020b, January 10). Why mind mapping works: The benefits of mind mapping. AYOA. https://www.ayoa.com/ourblog/why-mind-mapping-works-the-benefits-of-mind-mapping/

Curtis, S. (2019, August 6). How growth mindset makes for better student writing. *Education Week.* https://www.edweek.org/teaching-learning/opinion-how-growth-mindset-makes-for-better-student-writing/2019/08

Czajka, B. (2020, October 15). *What forms of media make the most money?* globalEDGE. https://globaledge.msu.edu/blog/post/56910/what-forms-of-media-make-the-most-money-

DIY Science. (n.d.). *How to prepare for an earthquake.* Cal Academy. Retrieved October 29th, 2021, from https://www.calacademy.org/explore-science/how-to-prepare-for-an-earthquake

Dweck, C. (2016, January 13). What having a "growth mindset" actually means. *Harvard Business Review.* https://hbr.org/2016/01/what-having-a-growth-mindset-actually-means

Dweck, C. (2017). *Mindset.* Robinson.

Ephemeral New York. (2011, March 7). *When New York was officially named New Orange.* https://ephemeralnewyork.wordpress.com/2011/03/07/when-new-york-was-officially-named-new-orange/

Farrand, P., Hussain, F., & Hennessy, E. (2002). The efficacy of the "mind map" study technique. *Medical Education, 36*(5), 426–431.

Federal Emergency Management Agency. (2009, August). *Personal preparedness in America: Findings from the 2009 Citizen Corps national survey.* https://s3-us-gov-west-1.amazonaws.com/dam-production/uploads/20130726-1859-25045-2081/2009_citizen_corps_national_survey_findings___full_report.pdf

Fleming, G. (2019a, July 3). *The ultimate guide to the 5-paragraph essay.* ThoughtCo. https://www.thoughtco.com/write-a-five-paragraph-essay-1856993

Fleming, G. (2019b, August 15). *How to write a personal narrative.* ThoughtCo. https://www.thoughtco.com/how-to-write-a-personal-narrative-1856809

Friedman, L. (2018, December 4). *7 key takeaways from* What the Health. Forks Over Knives. https://www.forksoverknives.com/wellness/7-key-takeaways-from-what-the-health/

Gambini, B. (2020, April 9). *Study: Money can't buy love—or friendship.* News Center, University at Buffalo. https://www.buffalo.edu/news/releases/2020/04/014.html

Gardiner, J. (n.d.). *Tapping into the subconscious.* Oxford Open Learning. https://www.oxfordhomeschooling.co.uk/blog/tapping-into-the-subconscious/

Gigasavvy. (2014, October 14). *How to use the rule of three to create better marketing content.* https://www.gigasavvy.com/how-to-use-the-rule-of-three-to-create-better-marketing-content/

Goodnough, K., & Woods, R. (2002, April 1–5). *Student and teacher perceptions of mind mapping: A middle school case study.* [Presentation]. American Educational Research Association Annual Meeting, New Orleans, LA, United States.

Greene, J. (n.d.). *Seven research-backed benefits of mind mapping.* Mindmeister. Retrieved October 28, 2021, from https://www.mindmeister.com/blog/mind-mapping-benefits-who-needs-mind-maps/

Gross, A. (2016, February 25). *87 percent of drivers engage in unsafe behaviors while behind the wheel.* AAA Newsroom. https://newsroom.aaa.com/2016/02/87-percent-of-drivers-engage-in-unsafe-behaviors-while-behind-the-wheel/

Harackiewicz, J. M., Smith, J. L., & Priniski, S. J. (2018). Interest matters: The importance of promoting interest in education. *Policy Insights from the Behavioural and Brain Sciences, 3*(2), 220–227. https://doi.org/10.1177/2372732216655542

History.com. (2021, September 15). *World War II.* https://www.history.com/topics/world-war-ii/world-war-ii-history

History.com (2022, March 22). *Benjamin Franklin.* https://www.history.com/topics/american-revolution/benjamin-franklin

Hoff, J. (2015, March 30). Engaging students with a mobile app. *Educause Review.* https://er.educause.edu/articles/2015/3/engaging-students-with-a-mobile-app

Holland, B., Holland, L., & Davies, J. (2003). An investigation into the concept of mind mapping and the use of mind mapping software to support and improve student academic performance. *Learning and Teaching Projects,* 89–94.

Holocaust Encyclopedia. (n.d.). *The Nazi rise to power.* United States Holocaust Memorial Museum. Retrieved March 25, 2022, from https://encyclopedia.ushmm.org/content/en/article/the-nazi-rise-to-power

Insurance Information Institute. (n.d.). *Facts and statistics: Teen drivers.* Retrieved October 28, 2021, from https://www.iii.org/fact-statistic/facts-statistics-teen-drivers

Insurance Journal. (2021, June 15). *Study says earthquakes are increasing in U.S. oil regions.* https://www.insurancejournal.com/news/national/2021/06/15/618657.htm

IvyPanda. (2019, September 26). *Importance of social interaction to learning essay (critical writing)*. https://ivypanda.com/essays/importance-of-social-interaction-to-learning-critical-writing/

Jones, R.C., Jr. (2019, March 14). *How do tornados and hurricanes compare?* News@TheU. https://news.miami.edu/stories/2019/03/how-do-tornadoes-and-hurricanes-compare.html

JRE Library. (2017, December 11). *Benefits of reading: Why you should read more.* https://jrelibrary.com/articles/benefits-of-reading-why-you-should-read-more/

Katz, A. (2008, April 27). *Only sure way to cut fatalities is to raise age, experts say.* UConn Health Today. https://today.uchc.edu/headlines/2008/apr08/raise_age.html

Kittelstad, K. (n.d.). *Five benefits of an essay outline.* Your Dictionary. Retrieved October 28, 2021, from https://grammar.yourdictionary.com/grammar/writing/benefits-of-an-essay-outline.html

Lange, D. (2020, December 11). *Recreational fishing in the U.S.: Statistics and facts.* Statista. https://www.statista.com/topics/1163/recreational-fishing/#dossierKeyfigures

Lee, T. B. (2014, September 1). *75 years ago, Hitler invaded Poland. Here's how it happened.* Vox. https://www.vox.com/2014/9/1/6084029/hitlers-invasion-of-poland-explained

Lexico. (n.d.). Peace. In *Lexico English Dictionary* powered by Oxford. Retrieved March 25, 2022, from https://www.lexico.com/definition/peace

LiveScience. (2008, March 3). *Students feel safer when armed with cell phone.* NBC. https://www.nbcnews.com/health/health-news/students-feel-safer-when-armed-cell-phone-flna1c9461554

Lo, J., & Hyland, F. (2007). Enhancing students' engagement and motivation in writing: The case of primary students in Hong Kong. *Journal of Second Language Writing, 16,* 219–237. https://doi.org/10.1016/j.jslw.2007.06.002

Lo Basso, F. (2020, September 21). *How reading fiction can shape our real lives. Greater Good Magazine.* https://greatergood.berkeley.edu/article/item/how_reading_fiction_can_shape_our_real_lives

Lozano, R., Naghavi, M., Foreman, K., Lim, S., Shibuya, K., Aboyans, V., Abraham, J., Adair, T., Aggarwal, R., Ahn, S.Y., AlMazroa, M.A., Alvarado, M., Anderson, H.R., Anderson, L.M., Andrews, K.G., Atkinson, C., Baddour, L.M., Barker-Collo, S., Bartels, D.H., . . . Lopez, A.D. (2012, December 15). Global and regional mortality from 235 causes of death for 20 age groups in 1990 and 2010: A systematic analysis for the Global Burden of Disease Study 2010. *The Lancet, 380*(9859), 2095–2128. https://doi.org/10.1016/S0140-6736(12)61728-0

MacArthur, C., & Moxley, J. (2020, August 12). *Growth mindset.* Writing Commons. https://writingcommons.org/section/mindset/growth-mindset/

MasterClass Staff. (2021, August 18). *Become a better writer by reading: Five ways reading improves writing.* MasterClass. https://www.masterclass.com/articles/become-a-better-writer-by-reading#5-ways-reading-improves-your-writing

MasterClass Staff. (2022, February 25). *Persuasive essay guide: How to write a persuasive essay*. MasterClass. https://www.masterclass.com/articles/persuasive-essay-guide#what-is-a-persuasive-essay

Matthews, J. (2020). *How to write a 5-paragraph essay step-by-step*.

Mayo Clinic. (n.d.). *Omega-3 in fish: How eating fish helps your heart*. Retrieved March 25, 2022, from https://www.mayoclinic.org/diseases-conditions/heart-disease/in-depth/omega-3/art-20045614

Miami Dade College. (2005, July). *Transitional words and phrases: Showing relationships within and between sentences*. MDC Kendall Campus College Prep. https://www.mdc.edu/kendall/collegeprep/documents2/transitional%20words%20and%20phrasesrevised815.pdf

Meyer, B., Haywood, N., Sachdev, D., & Faraday, S. (2008). *What is independent learning and what are the benefits for students?* Department for Children, Schools, and Families Research.

Modern Language Association Style Center. (2020, December 24). *Improving student writing through reading strategies*. https://style.mla.org/reading-strategies-and-writing/

National Geographic. (2021, May 3). *California's 7.1 earthquake–and how earthquakes work*. https://www.nationalgeographic.com/environment/article/earthquakes

National Health Service. (2020, March 10). *Prevention: Coronary heart disease*. https://www.nhs.uk/conditions/coronary-heart-disease/prevention/

Network Support. (n.d.). *Why use graphic organizers in the classroom?* Professional Learning Board. Retrieved October 28, 2021, from https://k12teacherstaffdevelopment.com/tlb/why-use-graphic-organizers-in-the-classroom/

North Carolina State University. (2021, October 25). *Writing assessment of non-native English speakers*. https://global.ncsu.edu/teaching-international-students/assessing-writing/assessing-writing-for-non-native-english-speakers/

OnHealth. (2008, July 29). *Earthquake preparedness: Emergency plan*. https://www.onhealth.com/content/1/earthquake_preparedness_emergency_plan

Osmun, R. (2022, March 15). *Oversleeping: The effects and health risks of sleeping too much*. Amerisleep. https://amerisleep.com/blog/oversleeping-the-health-effects/

Photinos, C. (n.d.). *Paragraph transitions*. Writing Commons. Retrieved March 25, 2022, from https://writingcommons.org/section/organization/paragraphs/paragraph-transitions/

Pottermore. (2018, February 1). *500 million Harry Potter books have now been sold worldwide*. Wizarding World. https://www.wizardingworld.com/news/500-million-harry-potter-books-have-now-been-sold-worldwide

Purdue Writing Lab. (n.d.-a). *Brainstorm for the essay*. Retrieved October 28, 2021, from https://owl.purdue.edu/engagement/ged_preparation/part_2_lessons_1_5/index.html

Purdue Writing Lab. (n.d.-b). *MLA style introduction*. Retrieved March 25, 2022, from https://owl.purdue.edu/owl/research_and_citation/mla_style/mla_style_introduction.html

Purdue Writing Lab. (n.d.-c). *Expository essays*. Retrieved March 25, 2022, from https://owl.purdue.edu/owl/general_writing/academic_writing/essay_writing/expository_essays.html

Silverman, D.J. (n.d.). Thanksgiving Day. *Britannica*. Retrieved March 25, 2022, from https://www.britannica.com/topic/Thanksgiving-Day

Study.com. (2022, January 18). *Mammals vs. reptiles*. https://study.com/academy/lesson/mammals-vs-reptiles.html

Teachnology, Inc. (n.d.) *Five reasons kids need homework and five reasons they don't*. Retrieved October 28, 2021, from https://www.teach-nology.com/tutorials/teaching/proandconhomework.html

Tesco Mobile. (2017, August 18). *Three ways mobile phones can help teens explore their independence*. Mashable. https://mashable.com/ad/article/mobile-phone-usage-for-teens

The Writing Center. (2009, June). *Five-paragraph essay*. Jackson State Community College. https://www.jscc.edu/academics/programs/writing-center/writing-resources/five-paragraph-essay.html

The Writing Center @PVCC. (2017). *Making a claim*. Piedmont Virginia Community College. https://www.pvcc.edu/files/making_a_claim.pdf

Traffis, C. (n.d.). *Learn the types of writing: Expository, descriptive, persuasive, and narrative*. Grammarly. Retrieved March 25, 2022, from https://www.grammarly.com/blog/types-of-writing/

Tuso, P. J., Ismail, M. H., Ha, B. P., & Bartolotto, C. (2013, Spring). Nutritional update for physicians: Plant-based diets. *The Permanente Journal, 17*(2), 61–66. https://doi.org/10.7812/TPP/12-085

University of Arizona. (2021, December 8). *MLA versus APA format*. https://www.uagc.edu/blog/mla-versus-apa-format

University of Illinois Extension. (n.d.) *Turkey Facts*. Retrieved March 25, 2022, from https://web.extension.illinois.edu/turkey/turkey_facts.cfm

University of Rochester Medical Center. (n.d.). *Burns overview*. Health Encyclopedia. Retrieved March 25, 2022, from https://www.urmc.rochester.edu/encyclopedia/content.aspx?ContentTypeID=90&ContentID=P01737

U.S. Department of the Interior. (2016, November 30). *Earthquakes in history*. https://pubs.usgs.gov/gip/earthq1/history.html

Vedantu. (2021, March 29). *What is the function of water in photosynthesis?* https://www.vedantu.com/question-answer/function-of-water-in-photosynthesis-class-11-biology-cbse-606299dc6a9fe969b7758123

Walshe, E. (2017, November 20). *The developing brain and teen driving*. Children's Hospital of Philadelphia. https://injury.research.chop.edu/blog/posts/developing-brain-and-teen-driving

Wilson, C., Ekhteraei, S., & Bevan, N. (n.d.). *Brainwriting*. Usability Body of Knowledge. Retrieved October 28, 2021, from https://www.usabilitybok.org/brainwriting

Weisman, K., Johnson, M.V., & Shutts, K. (2014, December 7). Young children's automatic encoding of social categories. *Developmental Science, 18*(6), 1036–1043. https://doi.org/10.1111/desc.12269

Wepler, R. (2013). *Composing an effective title.* Yale Writing Center. https://poorvucenter.yale.edu/sites/default/files/files/Titles%20(revised).pdf

Western Oregon University. (2020, December 14). *Chicago style guide, for 17th edition: Author-date references.* Hamersly Library. https://research.wou.edu/c.php?g=551307&p=3784519

World Health Organization. (2015, October 26). *Cancer: Carcinogenicity of the consumption of red meat and processed meat.* https://www.who.int/news-room/questions-and-answers/item/cancer-carcinogenicity-of-the-consumption-of-red-meat-and-processed-meat

Wright, N., Wilson, L., Smith, M., Duncan, B., & McHugh, P. (2017, March 20). The BROAD study: A randomized controlled trial using a whole food plant-based diet in the community for obesity, ischemic heart disease or diabetes. *Nutrition & Diabetes, 7*(3), e256. https://doi.org/10.1038/nutd.2017.3

WriteMyEssay4Me.org. (2021, May 27). *4 main types of essays in academic writing: Key features and samples.* https://writemyessay4me.org/blog/5-different-types-of-essays

Yang, M., Kenfield, S.A., Van Blarigan, E., Batista, J.L., Sesso, H.D., Ma, J., Stampfer, M.J., & Chavarro, J.E. (2015, May 31). Dietary patterns after prostate cancer diagnosis in relation to disease-specific and total mortality. *Cancer Prevention Research, 8*(6), 545–551. https://doi.org/10.1158/1940-6207.CAPR-14-0442

Zile, S.V. (2006). *Mastering the 5-paragraph essay.* Scholastic.

Answer Key

Chapter 1 Comprehension Quiz

1) d
2) d
3) a
4) b
5) d
6) c
7) d
8) c
9) b
10) a

Lesson 2.1 Exercise

Table 1) Food> Fruit> **Berries> The benefits of eating berries**

Sports> **Sports in the United States> Non-contact sports in the United States>** The most popular non-contact sport in the United States> **Question: What is the most popular non-contact sport in the United States? Statement: Discuss the most popular non-contact sport in the United States.**

Table 2) *example answer* Hobbies> **Singing> Opera> The history of opera in Australia> Question: What is the history of opera in Australia? Statement: Discuss the history of opera in Australia.**

example answer Technology> **Phones> Mobile apps on phones> The most used mobile app > Question: What is the most used mobile app today? Statement: Explain what the most used mobile app today is.**

example answer Education> **School> High school> The inadequacy of high school language departments> Question: Why do high school language departments fail to adequately teach students a foreign language?**

Statement: Discuss why high school language departments may be inadequate.

Table 3) *example answer* Countries> **Italy> Italian food> The history of pizza in Rome> Question: What is the history of pizza in Rome. Statement: Discuss the history of pizza in Rome.**

example answer Movies> **Romantic movies> Romantic Bollywood movies> The most popular romantic Bollywood movie> Question: What is the most popular romantic Bollywood movie? Statement: Explain what the most popular romantic Bollywood movie is and why.**

example answer Science> **cells> organelles> the role of mitochondria> Question: What is the role of mitochondria? Statement: Describe the role of mitochondria.**

Lesson 2.2 Exercise

2) **Subject Words:** life cycle of a frog
Command Word(s): describe

The command word is asking you to give a detailed description about the life cycle of a frog.

3) **Subject Words:** historical events that triggered the American Revolution
Command Word(s): No command word. This means you have to explain your thoughts.

There is no command word, so this means you have to explain your thoughts.

4) **Subject Words:** effects of eating healthy food versus junk food
Command Word(s): compare and contrast

The command words are asking you to show how two things (health food and junk food) are similar and how they are different.

5) **Subject Words:** the effects of smoking on physical health
Command Word(s): describe

The command word is asking you to give a detailed description of the effects of smoking on physical health.

Lesson 2.3 Exercise

1) e- parents
2) g- classmates
3) a- principal
4) c- local council
5) f- school cook
6) b- boss
7) d- sibling

Lesson 2.6 Exercise

1) **Subject Words:** the negative impact of texting while driving
Claim: Texting while driving is dangerous.

2) **Subject Words:** effects of weather on mood; pros and cons
Claim: Weather changes cause a change in mood.

3) **Subject Words:** the color of someone's bedroom walls affects their mental health
Claim: Bedroom color does affect mental health.

4) **Subject Words:** how technology reduces time spent outdoors
Claim: Technology reduces time spent outdoors.

5) **Subject Words:** natural remedies and modern medicine
Claim: Modern medicine is more effective than natural remedies.

6) **Subject Words:** social media protect young people
Claim: Social media does protect young people.

Lesson 2.7 Exercise

1) **Supporting Point 1:** It causes lung damage.
Supporting Point 2: It increases the risk of blood clots.
Supporting Point 3: It makes the immune system weaker.
(Centers for Disease Control and Prevention [CDC], 2021b)

2) **Supporting Point 1:** The leaves on trees change color.
Supporting Point 2: Fall is apple picking season.
Supporting Point 3: Everything comes in pumpkin spice flavor.

3) **Supporting Point 1:** Vegetables contain lots of vitamins and minerals.
Supporting Point 2: A vegetarian diet typically has fewer calories.
Opposing Point: Vitamin B12 is more readily available in a meat diet than in a meat-free diet.

4) **Supporting Point 1:** Practicing a skill helps learning.
Supporting Point 2: It helps store information in long-term memory.
Supporting Point 3: It creates habit and strengthens talent.

5) **Supporting Point 1:** It improves communication skills.
Supporting Point 2: It reduces loneliness.
Supporting Point 3: It increases memory capacity.

Answer Key

Lesson 2.7 Exercise II

1) a- supports
2) b- opposes
3) c- not relevant
4) b- opposes
5) a- supports
6) a- supports
7) b- opposes
8) c- not relevant

Lesson 2.8 Exercise

1) Possible Thesis Statement: Some people work harder than others because they are more motivated to reach the top of the ladder, they have to provide for others, and they have a more positive attitude toward work.

2) Possible Thesis Statement: Students should take a gap year to travel after college because it increases self-awareness, boosts confidence and communication skills, and helps develop an understanding of other cultures.

3) Possible Thesis Statement: Grades should be replaced with a pass/fail system because it would be less stressful for students and reduce the competition between classmates. However, having no grades may lead to lower motivation.

4) Possible Thesis Statement: There are several life skills more important than others, including communication and interpersonal skills, problem-solving and decision-making, and self-awareness and empathy.

5) Possible Thesis Statement: Mammals and reptiles are very different because mammals have hair, four-chambered hearts, and live births, while reptiles have scales, three-chambered hearts, and lay eggs.

Chapter 2 Comprehension Quiz

1) d
2) d
3) b
4) a
5) d
6) d
7) d
8) c
9) b
10) d

Chapter 3 Comprehension Quiz

1) a
2) d
3) d
4) d
5) d
6) a
7) c
8) d
9) d
10) d

Lesson 4.1.1 Exercise

Hook 2) *example answer*
Type of Hook: Short explanation of the essay topic's importance
New and Improved: Family enriches life and provides protection.

Hook 3) *example answer*
Type of Hook: Shocking fact/statistic
New and Improved: Approximately one fifth of U.S. females die from heart disease (Centers for Disease Control and Prevention, 2020).

Hook 4) *example answer*
Type of Hook: Fascinating question
New and Improved: What makes students successful?

Hook 5) *example answer*
Type of Hook: Contradiction
New and Improved: Fitness is a dream goal for most, yet we're reluctant to work for it.

Hook 6) *example answer*
Type of Hook: Clever quote
New and Improved: "A smile starts on the lips," according to Carolyn Birmingham.

Hook 7) *example answer*
Type of Hook: Fascinating question
New and Improved: Dogs are the number one pet in the U.S.; you can find them in almost 40% of all households!

Hook 8) *example answer*
Type of Hook: Short explanation of the essay topic's importance
New and Improved: The observable outer space is around 93 billion light-years in diameter, so it's worth paying attention to (Britannica, n.d.).

Hook 9) *example answer*
Type of Hook: Contradiction
New and Improved: For humans, safety is paramount, yet 45% of U.S. drivers speed while driving (Gross, 2016).

Lesson 4.1.2 Exercise

1) Statistic
2) Opinion
3) Relevant history
4) Current events
5) Definition
6) Fact

End-of-Lesson 4.1 Exercise

1) Hook: Underline sentence 1; **Background Information:** Circle sentences 2, 3, and 4; **Thesis Statement:** Squiggly line under sentence 5

2) Hook: Underline sentence 1; **Background Information:** Circle sentences 2, 3, and 4; **Thesis Statement:** Squiggly line under sentence 5

3) Hook: Underline sentence 1; **Background Information:** Circle sentence 2; **Thesis Statement:** Squiggly line under sentence 3

4) Hook: Underline sentence 1; **Background Information:** Circle sentences 2 and 3; **Thesis Statement:** Squiggly line under sentence 4

Lesson 4.2.1 Exercise

1) *example answer* **Topic Sentence 1:** Having fun and playing is an important aspect of childhood because it promotes the development of fine motor skills.
Topic Sentence 2: Childhood play is essential because it teaches children how to problem-solve.
Topic Sentence 3: Playing games during childhood helps build social interaction skills, which are useful later in life.

2) *example answer* **Topic Sentence 1:** Teenagers should have their own rooms because they need privacy.
Topic Sentence 2: It's important for teenagers to have their own rooms because they need quiet time to relax and wind down.
Topic Sentence 3: Teenagers should have their own rooms because it promotes independence, which is important for individual growth.

3) *example answer* **Topic Sentence 1:** Popcorn is the best movie snack because of its divine, buttery goodness.
Topic Sentence 2: Popcorn always satisfies a salty craving, making it the best movie snack.
Topic Sentence 3: Lastly, popcorn makes for the best movie snack because nothing beats its crunchy exterior.

Answer Key

Lesson 4.2.2 Exercise

1) *example answer* The heart is a muscle, and any muscle benefits from exercise, such as walking. A stronger heart can pump more blood around the body with less effort (National Health Service [NHS], 2020).

2) *example answer* Road safety campaigns teach drivers to wear a seatbelt while driving, to follow the speed limit, and to abide by the rules of the road. Otherwise, motor vehicle accidents and other road mishaps are more likely to occur.

3) *example answer* When children are allowed to trick-or-treat, they have a chance to get dressed up, go outside, and be physically active from all the walking between houses. They are able to run around and breathe fresh air, instead of being glued to their phones at home.

4) *example answer* The lead in mechanical pencils stays a consistent size and does not become dull, while the lead in wooden pencils dulls over time and needs to be regularly sharpened.

Lesson 4.2.3 Exercise

1) *example answer* Pumping blood around the heart with less effort is associated with reduced blood pressure and, therefore, a reduced risk of heart disease. When the heart has a difficult time pumping blood around the body, it's an indication of high blood pressure or plaque in the arteries. Both are associated with heart disease and a weak heart.

2) *example answer* If current road safety campaigns are successful in their mission to educate people and make

them more aware of risks, then drivers are less likely to make rash decisions and take risks while driving. They will err on the side of caution to make sure safety standards are met.

3) *example answer* Technology can often be a barrier to participating in more physical activities. Trick-or-treating is an opportunity for children to be outside and away from the screens in the house, where they are likely not getting the exercise they need.

4) *example answer* Because mechanical pencils never become dull, writers do not have to worry about their writing becoming illegible, a frequent concern when using wooden pencils. They can write with one less worry on their minds.

Lesson 4.2.4 Exercise

1) c
2) a
3) b
4) c

Lesson 4.2.5 Exercise

1) *example answer* **Possible Counterargument:** PCs are more powerful than Macs. **Analysis:** Although PCs are often more powerful, Macs are simpler to use, especially for someone who is new to computers.

2) *example answer* **Possible Counterargument:** Opening a bank account for children too soon is stressful. **Analysis:** Though it might sound overwhelming for kids to be responsible for money so early on, their parents can manage the account until their child seems ready to take more ownership.

3) *example answer* **Possible Counterargument:** Gym classes are poorly run and don't help students. **Analysis:** While some gym classes are poorly run and might not help students become superstar athletes, they should still be a mandatory part of the curriculum to get all students physically active in school.

End-of-Lesson 4.2 Exercise

1) **Topic Sentence:** Underline sentence 1; **Evidence:** Circle sentence 2; **Analysis:** Rectangle around sentences 3 and 4; **Concluding Sentence:** Squiggly line under sentence 5

2) **Topic Sentence:** Underline sentence 1; **Evidence:** Circle sentence 2; **Analysis:** Rectangle around sentences 3 and 4; **Concluding Sentence:** Squiggly line under sentence 5

3) **Topic Sentence:** Underline sentence 1; **Evidence:** Circle sentence 2; **Analysis:** Rectangle around sentences 3 and 4; **Concluding Sentence:** Squiggly line under sentence 5

4) **Topic Sentence:** Underline sentence 1; **Evidence:** Circle sentence 2; **Analysis:** Rectangle around sentence 3; **Concluding Sentence:** Squiggly line under sentence 4

Lesson 4.3.1 Exercise

1) *example answer* **Rephrased Thesis Statement:** Removing bad habits from your life is not a simple, one-step process. You must take a motivated approach by recognizing what

you want to change, replacing your bad habit with a good habit, and letting yourself make mistakes.

2) *example answer* **Rephrased Thesis Statement:** Fathers should be given the same duration of leave as mothers after the birth of a child because it is an important time for building a relationship and providing support.

3) *example answer* **Rephrased Thesis Statement:** There are many differences between cities and rural areas. The three factors accounting for the biggest differences are population, buildings, and green space availability.

4) *example answer* **Rephrased Thesis Statement:** School uniforms have a negative emotional and financial impact; they do not have any beneficial effect on learning, so there is no reason for them to be required.

5) *example answer* **Rephrased Thesis Statement:** Lying can ruin your relationship with others and yourself, as it damages trust, makes people upset, and threatens your values and morals.

Lesson 4.3.2 Exercise

1) *example answer* **Wrap Up and Review:** While making a plan and having a strategy in place keeps you prepared and mitigates panic, identifying safe spaces allows you to respond quicker. And, of course, emergency supplies ensure you have everything you need, exactly when you need it.

Answer Key

2) *example answer* **Wrap Up and Review:** Taking care of one's physical and mental health is crucial, especially during formative years and adolescence. Though the positive environmental impact of riding a bike is generally seen as just a bonus, the environment cannot be treated as an afterthought.

3) *example answer* **Wrap Up and Review:** Collaborating with others and seeing document edit history are much more seamless processes in Google Docs than they are in Microsoft Word. Additionally, what Google Docs lacks in tables and graphs, it more than makes up for with its user-friendly design.

Lesson 4.3.3 Exercise

1) *example answer* **Closing Statement:** In order to enjoy vibrant health and optimal energy, humans must consume carbohydrates; they should not be removed from the human diet, or there will be consequences to pay.

2) *example answer* **Closing Statement:** Checking for these three qualities in a person can help you decide if they will be a part of your life and can ensure you will not get hurt if you decide to be a part of their life.

3) *example answer* **Closing Statement:** Sometimes, our perspectives can change when we try to see a situation from others' viewpoints. Would your friend prefer you respond to their text immediately, or would they rather know you made it to your destination safely?

End-of-Lesson 4.3 Exercise

1) **Rephrased Thesis Statement:** Underline sentence 1; **Wrap Up and Review:** Circle sentences 2 and 3; **Closing Statement:** Squiggly line under sentence 4

2) **Rephrased Thesis Statement:** Underline sentences 1 and 2; **Wrap Up and Review:** Circle sentence 3; **Closing Statement:** Squiggly line under sentence 4

3) **Rephrased Thesis Statement:** Underline sentences 1 and 2; **Wrap Up and Review:** Circle sentence 3; **Closing Statement:** Squiggly line under sentence 4

4) **Rephrased Thesis Statement:** Underline sentence 1; **Wrap Up and Review:** Circle sentence 2; **Closing Statement:** Squiggly line under sentence 3

Lesson 4.4 Exercise

1) a; opposing
2) b; summary
3) d; agreement
4) d; opposing
5) a; causal
6) c; sequence
7) c; opposing
8) d; causal

Lesson 4.5 Exercise

1) *possible answer* Enacting Change to Combat Climate Change
2) *possible answer* Self-Love Isn't Narcissism
3) *possible answer* Navigating the World on Your Own Terms
4) *possible answer* A Thorough Description of What You Should do in a Meteor Shower

5) *possible answer* An Analysis of Small Businesses During the Covid-19 Pandemic
6) *possible answer* I Don't Understand: How to Be a Better Listener and Ask the Right Questions
7) *possible answer* Dreaming Big: Fiction's Effect on Children and Their Aspirations

Lesson 4.6 Exercise

1) b
2) a
3) a
4) b
5) b
6) trick question; no right answer
7) b
8) a
9) trick question; no right answer

Chapter 4 Comprehension Quiz

1) d
2) c
3) a
4) b
5) b
6) c
7) b
8) d
9) d
10) d

Lesson 5.1 Exercise

1) yes
2) no
3) no
4) yes
5) yes

Lesson 5.1 Exercise II

1) *possible answer* **Is the language consistent? Explain your answer.**
Yes. Each sentence talks about burns, which is what the prompt focuses on. Additionally, every sentence talks about the impact of burns on the body, which is what the prompt asks for.

Does the language flow nicely? Explain your answer.
The language flows nicely because it focuses on the same topic, and each sentence makes sense in relation to the sentence before and after it.
Give one word to describe the topic of the paragraph.
Scars

2) *possible answer* **Is the language consistent? Explain your answer.**
No. The language focuses on the sun in the first sentence. Then, it immediately changes focus to water for the majority of the rest of the paragraph. This is an issue because many of the sentences do not relate back to the prompt.
Does the language flow nicely? Explain your answer.
No. Some wording in this paragraph is choppy and is phrased awkwardly. There are some unnecessary words and a few grammatical errors. The paragraph lacks fluidity, despite the attempt to use transitional phrases.
Give one word to describe the topic of the paragraph.
Water. This is not good because the main message should be about sunlight.

3) *possible answer* **Is the language consistent? Explain your answer.**
The paragraph does a good job of making sure each sentence relates back to the prompt. So, the message is consistent, even though the wording isn't the best.
Does the language flow nicely? Explain your answer.
The language does not flow very nicely. Transitions are not used effectively. The writing sounds undeveloped, coarse, and repetitive. There are wordy phrases and sentences.

Answer Key

Give one word to describe the topic of the paragraph.
Harry Potter

Lesson 5.2 Exercise

1) *possible answer* **Read the sentence out loud. Is it clear? Does it make sense? Does the language sound awkward? Explain your answer.**
The sentence does make sense, but it's longer than it needs to be. The language sounds awkward because there are too many unnecessary words.
Are there better words that can be used while keeping the same meaning?
Instead of "it is often the case that" you can say "often." Instead of "get on with each other" you can say "don't get along." The term "that" can also be deleted, since it's an unnecessary filler word.
Rewrite the sentence if you think it's necessary.
Often, cats and dogs don't get along.

2) *possible answer* **Read the sentence out loud. Is it clear? Does it make sense? Does the language sound awkward? Explain your answer.**
The sentence does make sense, but it has some unnecessary words that make it long and awkward.
Are there better words that can be used while keeping the same meaning?
"At this current moment in time" can be changed to "currently."
Rewrite the sentence if you think it's necessary.
Currently, more people watch TV than play video games.

3) *possible answer* **Read the sentence out loud. Is it clear? Does it make sense? Does the language sound awkward? Explain your answer.**

The sentence isn't fully clear, because of the confusing double negative and wordiness.
Are there better words that can be used while keeping the same meaning?
"You can't not agree" can be made into "you can't disagree." Change "when they are able to prove that you are wrong" to "who prove you wrong."
Rewrite the sentence if you think it's necessary.
You can't disagree with people who prove you wrong

4) *possible answer* **Read the sentence out loud. Is it clear? Does it make sense? Does the language sound awkward? Explain your answer.**
This sentence makes sense, but there are some words that can be removed or changed.
Are there better words that can be used while keeping the same meaning?
"Each and every time" can be rewritten to "Every time." "Certain" can be changed to "specific," which fits better in this sentence.
Rewrite the sentence if you think it's necessary.
Every time you recall a memory, you activate a specific part of your brain.

Lesson 5.3 Exercise

1) Omega-3 lowers blood pressure, looks after the heart, and reduces the likelihood of heart disease.
2) Eating breakfast will give you energy for the rest of the day.
3) Birds migrate across **the world** for winter.
4) She screamed, "don't do that," as he ran away.
5) **Evidence** shows there is a build up of magma in a volcano before it erupts.
6) The distance between **the** two stations **was** three miles.

7) **S**he spent her day swimming in the sea.
8) Samantha's dad had **run** out of patience.
9) Alex loves to **sell** homemade scarves.
10) The dog barked at **the** squirrel running **around outside.**

Lesson 5.3 Exercise II

My first experience with kindness was when my mom scooped me up as a child. I had tumbled over while sprinting towards an ice cream truck. She cradled me in her arms and sang a lullaby softly, while gently rocking me back and forth. I knew in that moment what kindness, warmth, and love felt like. Since then, I have looked for kindness in other people. However, there's nothing quite like the love of your parents/guardians; it's unconditional.
My second experience with kindness was from a friend. My cat had gone missing that weekend. I still remember the intense anxiety I felt. I was distracted in school and quiet when with my friends. One friend, Melissa, took me aside and checked up on me, saying she had noticed I was quiet. I told her about my cat. "It's normal for cats to go missing for a couple of days," she said. She reassured me that he would return soon. This act of kindness, Melissa noticing my frantic behavior and checking up on me, is something I'll always remember.

Chapter 5 Comprehension Quiz

1) d
2) c
3) d
4) d
5) d
6) b
7) d
8) b
9) d
10) a

Lesson 6.1 Exercise

1) b
2) a
3) a
4) b
5) b
6) b
7) a
8) b

Lesson 6.2 Exercise

1) personal
2) characters
3) voice
4) first
5) lesson
6) chronological
7) creativity
8) personal details

Lesson 6.3 Exercise

1) **Flamingo-** Pink, tall, long, beautiful
2) **Pizza-** Cheesy, salty, tangy, savory
3) **Sleepover-** Loud, noisy, fun
4) **Bed-** Soft, comfortable, warm, firm
5) **Castle-** Large, majestic, fancy, strong
6) **Garbage-** Large, majestic, fancy, strong
7) **Glass of Water-** Refreshing, cool, clean, cold
8) **Hugging-** Tight, comforting, relaxing, relieving
9) **An audience clapping-** Enthusiastic, loud, boisterous, rowdy
10) **Cat-** Soft, furry, squishy, hairy

Lesson 6.4 Exercise

1) a
2) b
3) b
4) a
5) b
6) b
7) a
8) a

<u>Answer Key</u>

<u>Chapter 6 Comprehension Quiz</u>

1) c
2) c
3) b
4) a
5) d
6) d
7) b
8) d
9) a
10) c

<u>Chapter 7 Comprehension Quiz</u>

1) d
2) c
3) a
4) d
5) d
6) c
7) d
8) b
9) d
10) b

Made in the USA
Las Vegas, NV
01 December 2024